Clear Speech

Pronunciation and Listening Comprehension in North American English

4th Edition

Teacher's Resource and Assessment Book

Judy B. Gilbert

CAMBRIDGE
UNIVERSITY PRESS

CAMBRIDGE
UNIVERSITY PRESS

32 Avenue of the Americas, New York, NY 10013-2473, USA

Cambridge University Press is part of the University of Cambridge.

It furthers the University's mission by disseminating knowledge in the pursuit of education, learning and research at the highest international levels of excellence.

www.cambridge.org

Information on this title: www.cambridge.org/9781107637061

© Cambridge University Press 2012

First published 1984
Second edition 1993
Third edition 2005
4th printing 2014

Printed in the United States of America

A catalog record for this publication is available from the British Library.

ISBN 978-1-107-68295-5 Student's Book
ISBN 978-1-107-63706-1 Teacher's Resource and Assessment Book
ISBN 978-1-107-62743-7 Class and Assessment Audio CDs

For a full list of components, visit www.cambridge.org/clearspeech

Art direction, book design, layout services, and photo research: Q2A/Bill Smith
Audio production: Richard LePage and Associates

"Lone Jack to Knob Noster" by Jack Rummel from his CD, Lone Jack: The Ragtime of Today.

Contents

Appendices

Extra Practice 1 - More Consonant Work

Extra Practice 2 - Advanced Tasks

Lectures for Listening Practice

Tests and Quizzes

Letter to the Teacher

From the very first edition, *Clear Speech* has concentrated on the way that musical signals of spoken English are used to show emphasis – that is, stress, vowel lengthening, and pitch change. If the emphasis signals are clear, English listeners will understand the message even if there are errors in individual sounds. Conversely, even if the sounds are fairly clear, errors in emphasis or stress might confuse the listener.

Now this fourth edition of *Clear Speech*, revised with valuable feedback from teachers, adds new support to help you teach your students these musical signals of spoken English. This letter outlines the new features of both the Student's Book and this Teacher's Resource and Assessment Book.

New Features of *Clear Speech*, Fourth Edition

A pronunciation pyramid adds new support.

This concept makes it easier for students to understand how the various aspects of spoken English work together.

The pyramid is divided into four levels, each with a distinctive color. (You will find the full-color pyramid on page x of the Student's Book.) The base, or foundation, level of the pyramid is the *thought group* (a short sentence, a clause, or a phrase). Within that base, there is a *focus word*, which is the most important word in the thought group. Within the focus word, there is one most *stressed syllable*. The vowel at the center of this syllable is the *peak vowel*, which is the top of the pyramid and the peak of information. Accuracy is necessary when pronouncing this vowel.

Throughout the Student's Book, the pyramid appears at appropriate points to remind students how the specific topic being taught fits into the whole system of spoken English. With the same purpose, Rules and Vowel Work boxes are shaded in the pyramid level color that corresponds to the topic being presented.

More support for vowel rules is given.

Sound symbols are used in specific tasks to help students recognize how pronunciation of sounds relates to the spelling rules. Also, the percentage of time these rules actually work is given directly with the practice tasks.

A color design adds visual appeal and clarity to presentation and practice.

A color design as well as updated illustrations and graphics make the presentations even clearer and provide more support for the practice tasks.

The audio program is available for students to download.

The complete audio program for the listening tasks in the Student's Book is available as MP3s on the website www.cambridge.org/clearspeech. Students can now download the audio for further practice outside the classroom.

An app with games makes self-study practice more engaging.

Four games with hundreds of activities provide further practice of key pronunciation aspects. The *Pronunciation: Clear Speech* App for iPhone, iPad, and iPod touch is available on the App Store.

Features of the Teacher's Resource and Assessment Book

This Teacher's Resource and Assessment Book includes the following features, all of which enhance the teaching of the Student's Book and help teachers manage their pronunciation lessons more effectively.

Unit overviews

Each unit begins with a description of its main teaching points, to facilitate class planning.

Task descriptions

These task descriptions include a variety of presentation ideas as well as useful theoretical background information. Tasks marked in the Teacher's Resource and Assessment Book by the headphones icon 🎧 are included on the Class Audio CDs. The CD and track numbers are also provided to help teachers quickly access the material on the Class Audio program.

Audio scripts

All of the material on the Class Audio program that does not appear on the pages of the Student's Book is presented in the audio scripts. Scripts for the "Which word do you hear?" and "Which word is different?" tasks contain phonetic transcriptions. Teachers can use the transcriptions as a pronunciation guideline when reading the items themselves or to help clarify the pronunciation of specific items for students. A key to the phonetic symbols used in the Teacher's Resource and Assessment Book can be found on pages xiv–xv.

Answer keys

All of the answers to tasks that require students to come up with specific responses are included. Suggested answers are also given for some of the open-ended tasks. These should help guide students that might have trouble coming up with their own answers for such tasks.

Teaching tips

These are expansion activities or further presentation ideas that reinforce or extend the points students are learning in the unit. They can add more fun and variety to the lessons.

Lectures

Lectures on topics relevant to pronunciation learning are included for additional listening comprehension practice.

Clear Listening Diagnostic Test and Clear Speaking Diagnostic Test

Both these photocopiable tests can be used either at the beginning of the course to determine which areas students need improvement or at the end of the course to provide students with a measure of their progress. The audio for the listening test is available on the Assessment Audio CD packed with the Class Audio CDs.

Pronunciation Profile Form

This photocopiable form can be used to evaluate students' performance in the Clear Speaking Diagnostic Test.

Unit quizzes

Photocopiable quizzes are provided for Units 1 through 15. The quizzes are designed to be given after the completion of each unit, and they have been revised and expanded for the fourth edition. The audio for the quizzes is available on the Assessment Audio CD.

Test and quizzes audio scripts and answer keys

This section includes the audio scripts and answer keys for all the tasks in the listening test and unit quizzes. It also indicates the Assessment Audio CD track number for the recording for each task. Directions for reading the test and quizzes tasks out loud for the students are also provided.

Glossary

The glossary defines terms used in the Student's Book in nontechnical language that is suitable for student comprehension.

Bibliography

The bibliography provides reference to information cited in the Teacher's Resource and Assessment Book. This can also be helpful as further reading for a teacher's own research.

Components of *Clear Speech,* Fourth Edition

Student's Book

The Student's Book makes understanding the key concepts of English pronunciation easier with simple and clear explanations, aided by a variety of oral, visual, and kinesthetic resources. Practical rules and a variety of practice activities help students improve their listening and speaking skills. Appendices at the end of the book provide useful reference material and extra practice for more advanced classes.

Teacher's Resource and Assessment Book

This book provides practical explanations for the rationale for each lesson, useful classroom procedures, teaching tips, more dictations, and short lectures for listening practice, as well as the audio script and answer key for each task. It also includes a listening diagnostic test, a speaking diagnostic test and a student's pronunciation profile form, 15 unit quizzes, and all the audio scripts and answer keys.

Class Audio and Assessment Audio CDs

This set includes three Class Audio CDs with the audio for all the listening tasks in the Student's Book and one Assessment Audio CD with the audio for all the tasks in the listening test and quizzes.

App

The App *Pronunciation: Clear Speech* is available for iPhone, iPad, and iPod touch. It includes hundreds of fun interactive activities for engaging practice with word stress, syllables, and beginning and final sounds. It is available on the App store.

Website

The website www.cambridge.org/clearspeech provides extra materials and information about the series, including the complete audio for all the listening activities in the Student's Book as downloadable MP3s.

I hope that you find using this fourth edition of *Clear Speech* to be an enjoyable and professionally rewarding experience.

Judy B. Gilbert

Introduction

This introduction explains the approach to pronunciation reflected in *Clear Speech*, Fourth Edition. It will help you understand why the book is organized as it is and why it emphasizes the "musical" aspects of English: rhythm, stress, and intonation. This introduction also presents some pedagogical reflections and recommendations that can help you make the most of your pronunciation lessons.

Linguistic underpinnings

Here is a sad story: A teacher has just completed a successful pronunciation lesson using minimal pairs of words to teach the sounds /r/ and /l/. All of the students were able to manage the distinction by the end of the lesson. The students feel good and the teacher feels good. Then, as the students are leaving the room, one student turns to the teacher and cheerfully says, "So rong!" The teacher does not feel so good anymore.

The fact is that minimal pair practice alone sometimes yields minimal results. This may be part of the reason that the teaching of pronunciation has fallen into disfavor in so many programs. Lack of success is discouraging to teachers, and students sometimes feel that pronunciation is an endless succession of unrelated and unmanageable pieces. If the work is so discouraging, shouldn't we just drop it? Why should we include pronunciation in the curriculum?

There are two fundamental reasons to teach pronunciation. First of all, students need to understand, and, secondly, they need to be understood. If they are not able to understand spoken English well, or if they cannot be understood easily, they are cut off from the language, except in its written form.

The relationship between speaking and listening comprehension

Intelligibility involves both speaking and listening comprehension. Following are two commonplace situations that, taken together, illustrate this fact. In the first situation, say in a bus station in an English-speaking country, a low-level student eagerly tries out something that has been carefully rehearsed in class, only to find out that the other person does not understand and even breaks off the interaction with a show of irritation. Native speakers are not necessarily unpleasant by nature, but they are often in a hurry and, unlike ESL/EFL teachers, they are not professionally patient. A few humiliating experiences like this one may make learners so discouraged that they give up trying. Such a student may continue to attend classes, but may also stop believing that there is much use in making an effort. And as you know, discouraged students are hard to teach.

Here is another situation, this time set in the workplace: A new employee, who is not a native speaker of English, is approached by a supervisor, who is a native speaker. The supervisor says something that sounds like, "It's very important to *schussel* the *wozzick*." The employee, not really understanding but eager to make a good impression, nods enthusiastically and says, "Important, yes, yes!" Later, the supervisor returns to find the task not done, or done incorrectly. What conclusion is apt to be reached? That the worker is dishonest? Stupid? Lazy? Unfortunately, few supervisors would realize that the problem came from inadequate listening comprehension. That is why English instruction must address the relationship between pronunciation and listening comprehension. This is true for students at every level, regardless of their proficiency in writing and reading English.

The relationship between rhythm and reading

Not known to many teachers, there is a bonus benefit to practicing speaking with English rhythm: a useful effect on learning to read in English. The reason for the effect is that rhythm affects the way people hear sounds. If the timing is wrong, it's hard to identify the sound accurately. Since people from other languages tend to hear and speak in the rhythm / timing of their first language, this can affect the clarity of their listening perception. And if you can't efficiently catch the clarity of sounds that make up words, research shows that it slows down your ability to tie sounds to letters in reading. For this reason, getting the new rhythm right can actually help students identify the sequence of sounds, a precondition to literacy in the target language that reading specialists refer to as *phonological awareness*. (David et al., 2007; Wade-Wooley &Wood, 2006; Wood, 2006; Goswami & Bryant, 1990).

Segmentals and suprasegmentals

There are two main components of pronunciation: the *segmentals* and the *suprasegmentals*. The word "segmentals" refers to individual sounds. For instance, look at the first lines of this song, a Canadian version of a popular U.S. folk song:

> This land is your land,
> This land is my land,
> From Bonavista to Vancouver Island.

If the sounds represented by the letters -l-, -b-, and -v- in these lines are not said correctly, intelligibility will be harmed. But suprasegmentals also affect intelligibility. The word "suprasegmentals" refers to the musical qualities of rhythm, stress, and intonation that carry the sounds along and help convey emphasis and coherence. For instance, in this song, it is important that extra length be given to the word "your" in the first line and "my" in the next line because this emphasis links the two words together to mean "yours and mine together." In English, suprasegmentals are mainly used to signal emphasis and the relationship between ideas.

Why are the suprasegmentals of a new language so important?

Following are two sentences that are almost identical.

a. We have a lot of money.
b. We had a lot of money.

The only difference between these sentences is a contrast of segmentals; that is, the final consonant sounds in "have" and "had" are different. Is this difference important? Yes, of course. But the other component, the suprasegmentals, must be considered as well. Consider, for example, how different emphasis patterns might change the meaning of each sentence. Emphasis on "had" in the second sentence, for instance, would imply that (regrettably) the situation has changed. Emphasis on other words would suggest different meanings.

Now consider the following sentences, which are also nearly identical.

a. John said, "The boss is late!"
b. "John," said the boss, "is late!"

Who was speaking in each sentence? When reading the sentences, the written punctuation marks let us know who was speaking. In the spoken form, however, there are no visible punctuation marks. Furthermore, practice distinguishing the individual sounds in each sentence would not help a learner understand the difference in meaning.

Intermediate students probably have learned to understand written punctuation, but they also need to recognize spoken punctuation – the suprasegmental signals that tell a listener how words are grouped.

This musical element is significant both for intelligibility and for effective listening comprehension.

One American teaching trainee had this to say at the end of a pronunciation methods course:

> When I began the class, I expected to learn techniques for teaching the individual sounds, but now I believe pronunciation is bigger than that. Now I think trying to teach somebody pronunciation without paying attention to the suprasegmentals is like teaching somebody ballroom dancing, only without music, without a partner, and standing still.

On reading this comment, a Japanese teacher in the class said, "You could also say that trying to learn English pronunciation without suprasegmentals is like trying to learn swimming on a *tatami* (straw mat) floor."

Alexander Graham Bell, who was deeply concerned with both hearing and intelligibility, wrote:

> Ordinary people who know nothing of phonetics or elocution have difficulties in understanding slow speech composed of perfect sounds, while they have no difficulty in comprehending an imperfect gabble if only the accent and rhythm are natural. (Bell, 1916)

In other words, when the suprasegmentals are right, the individual sound errors are more or less camouflaged. That is, the listener pays more attention to the emphasis than to the individual sounds. I would also add that the individual sounds have a better chance of being pronounced accurately if they are said with the right timing.

English uses suprasegmentals to help the listener follow the thoughts of the speaker – to know which words are important and how they are connected. Other languages tend to use other means to indicate which words are important and to show how ideas are related, but spoken English relies mainly on the suprasegmental cues of rhythm, stress, and intonation, the "music" of the spoken language.

Rhythm

Children learn the rhythm of their first language in the first months of life. By the age of six months to a year, they are deeply familiar with that rhythm and thereafter unconsciously apply it to any new language they learn. It is therefore strategically important to bring the system of English rhythm to students' conscious attention.

The topic of rhythm is introduced in Unit 1 of the Student's Book, where students learn about the basic unit of English rhythm: the syllable. The topic is thereafter spiraled throughout the remaining units, and English rhythm is practiced through many activity types designed to fit a variety of learning styles.

Stress patterns

Misplaced stress is one of the major sources of conversation breakdown. In fact, stress is so significant for intelligibility that English speakers systematically use several simultaneous signals of stress. The most crucial of these signals are *vowel lengthening* and *contrastive clarity*. English learners must be given ample opportunity to use the signals automatically, but these signals are best addressed one at a time.

Unit 3 of the Student's Book presents vowel lengthening, while Unit 4 presents contrastive clarity. Unit 5 provides practice with recognizing and using these signals concurrently. It also provides various simple rules for stress. Consolidation of stress cues will prepare students to learn about one of the most important topics in *Clear Speech: intonational emphasis*.

Intonational emphasis

Each English *thought group* (a short sentence, clause, or phrase) has a most-important word, called the *focus word*. This is the word that the speaker wants the listener to notice most. Unlike many languages, English depends mainly on intonation to help the listener notice the focus word. That is, by changing the pitch on the stressed syllable of a focus word, the speaker gives *emphasis* to that word and, thereby, highlights it for the listener. Because other languages use other means to call attention to the important idea, learners tend not to notice this specifically English system for signaling emphasis.

Emphasis and *focus* are the main topics of Units 6 through 9 in the Student's Book. The units leading up to Unit 6 are meant to develop the ability to stress some syllables while obscuring others. This contrast between stressed and reduced syllables is essential to drawing strong attention to the focus word in a given thought group.

For the sake of simplicity and learnability, the Student's Book initially discusses emphasis within the context of a sentence. That is, students learn that a sentence has one or more focus words, and they learn to identify and emphasize those focus words. Unit 15 of the Student's Book introduces the concept of the thought group. Students learn that a thought group may be a short sentence, a part of a sentence (a clause or phrase), or simply an incomplete remark. In that final unit, the topic of focus is integrated into work with these smaller parts of sentences.

Segmentals (vowels and consonants)

Although *Clear Speech* concentrates on rhythm, stress, and intonation, the Student's Book also gives a great deal of attention to individual sounds, both vowels and consonants. Students need to hear these sounds many times in order to be able to develop awareness of the boundaries which define the sounds; for example, the distinction between /æ/ as in "man," and /ɛ/ as in "men." When they have a clear acoustic image of the differences, they have an accurate mental inventory of English sounds to rely on when both speaking and listening.

Vowel sounds are presented early in the Student's Book (Unit 2) in order to prepare students for work with word stress. Since words are stressed by adding length and clarity to the vowel in a particular syllable, it is important for students to have good control of a basic set of English vowels if they are to practice English stress patterns. Additional vowel topics are dealt with in the Vowel Work sections at the end of later units.

Units 10 through 14 deal with topics related to consonant sounds. Once students have learned about the musical aspects of English, they will be prepared to practice the individual consonants more efficiently. That is because the target sounds are easier to produce and hear accurately when they are practiced in words and sentences with correct rhythm, stress, and intonation.

For more detailed information on the layout of the Student's Book, refer to the Scope and Sequence on pages vi–vii of that book, which highlights all of the major topics covered.

Pedagogical reflections

These are ideas I have collected over many years of teaching and talking to other pronunciation teachers. I hope that you find them useful.

The spoken language is different from the written language.

Most students assume that the written language and spoken language are identical. But in fact, there are many differences between written and spoken English. A vocabulary item is not really possessed until it is understood both in its printed form and in terms of its stress-affected spoken form.

Learning a second language is different from learning a first language.

Children learn to recognize the sounds and music of their first language within their first year of life. As part of that early learning process, they also learn to ignore the sounds and musical patterns that are not part of their mother tongue. In other words, they learn what to listen for and what not to listen for. For this reason, learning a second language involves not only becoming familiar with new sounds and melodies, but it also involves learning the ability to temporarily set aside sounds and patterns required for clarity in the first language. Some people seem to have an intuitive gift that allows them to pay attention to the sounds and music of a new language, but most students need to have these elements consciously brought to their attention since their first language is so deeply rooted in their psyche.

Pronunciation is very personal.

Good pronunciation in a new language requires a student, in a sense, to adopt a new persona. Some people find this easy to do, but most people do not. Many students tend to feel threatened by the idea of adopting the sounds and music of a new language. This is because the new sounds and different rhythm cause them to sound foreign to themselves. Typically, this reaction is not consciously recognized by the learner, but it is nonetheless a true barrier to adaptation. Teachers need to recognize that while grammar and vocabulary are difficult to learn, they do not present the same psychological difficulties for students as pronunciation. This is because the sounds and music of one's first language are learned so early that they are part of who we are and what group we belong to.

In some cases, students' discomfort with learning new pronunciation patterns may be so strong as to cause students to resist. Generally, this resistance manifests itself in a student not really absorbing what is being taught, or perhaps showing impatience or boredom. If the teacher or the other students get impatient with the uneasy learner, progress inevitably becomes even more difficult. In fact, even kindly teachers can intimidate a threatened student simply by their eagerness to help, especially when that eagerness results in teaching too many points at a pace faster than the concepts can be absorbed.

In this Teacher's Resource and Assessment Book, I suggest several ways that teachers can reduce the effect of these psychological obstacles to learning English pronunciation.

Adults can improve their pronunciation.

Adults may not be as malleable as young people, and so their habitual speech may not change much. However, that does not mean they cannot benefit from knowing how to fix a breakdown in communication if lack of intelligibility causes trouble in a particular situation.

"Accent addition" is better than "accent reduction."

The psychological difference between these two expressions is that instead of concentrating on erasing an accent, it is better to think about helping students add a different way of saying something when they have a practical reason to communicate with native speakers

Conscientious teachers often ask, "How can we reduce student errors?" It is useful to turn that question around and ask, "How can we increase student clarity?" Instead of trying to remove mispronunciation, which is often simply a transfer of something from the first language, it is more helpful for teachers to concentrate on adding new elements required by the target language.

The workload should be limited to what actually can be achieved.

If a task seems to be extra difficult, consider putting it off until the class has been refreshed by an activity they can complete successfully. This can help build a rising momentum of confidence, and a confident student is better able to learn.

Time is short, so priority topics are enough for now.

Teachers naturally want their students to achieve great clarity of speech in a relatively short time. There are two problems with this natural tendency:

a. Pronunciation improvement tends to be slow and not regular.

b. An overloaded student tends not to learn anything well.

For these reasons, it is better to restrict the topics to be mastered to those elements that are most important for intelligibility and listening comprehension. Each element should be practiced through different types of tasks until it is solidly learned. Later, when students have a solid foundation in these elements, they can be taught more subtle aspects of pronunciation.

Nervousness has a negative effect on pronunciation.

Nervousness tends to develop when students feel they are slipping behind others or when they feel that they are under too much pressure to perform well. Such nervousness has an especially negative effect on pronunciation. It is generally hard, for instance, for students to be courageous when called on to recite words or phrases alone. For this reason, it is preferable to have students recite words and phrases in chorus with the rest of the class (see the section on Quality Repetition below). Another way to lessen student tension is to use pair work. This type of activity requires students to pay attention only to their partners and protects them from feeling like the focus of class awareness.

Variety helps.

Students need a lot of practice to fix rhythm and other elements of pronunciation into their physical memory. However, extended drills can become boring, and boredom causes students' attention to wander. In order to get enough practice without getting the "vacant stare" effect, it is necessary to vary activities as much as possible, all the while continuing work on the same topic. For this reason, each unit in *Clear Speech* includes a variety of activity types. Following are descriptions of some of these activity types.

Listening tasks

Focused listening activities provide a solid foundation for confident, accurate speaking. The "Which word do you hear?" and "Which word is different?" tasks that appear throughout the Student's Book, for instance, help students learn to recognize and distinguish between particular sounds and stress patterns. These tasks also prepare students for the speaking activities that follow.

Pair work

Pair work activities provide a communicative challenge and give students – even in very large classes – the opportunity to practice speaking and hearing English. These activities also provide the immediate feedback so important to motivation. Moreover, they place more responsibility for learning where it belongs – with the student.

Dictation

Taking dictation alerts students to areas of listening perception that still need improvement. In addition to the dictation activities that appear throughout the Student's Book, you may also want to create your own dictation exercises using words from other activities (e.g., listening activities or dialogues).

Kinesthetic tasks

Having students move some part of their bodies (by raising a hand, a finger, or even just their eyebrows) or having them actually get up and move around the room, can help imprint a pronunciation element into students' physical memory. Put another way, kinesthetic work can help students physically internalize pronunciation elements such as rhythm and stress.

Music of English boxes

Learning the pronunciation of a second language is something like learning to play tennis. If you concentrate too much on trying to remember what to do with your wrist and, at the same time, try to remember how to position your feet, shoulders, and knees while also trying to remember to keep your eye on the ball, the combination of too many things to think about tends to keep you from putting everything together in a flowing movement. Although a tennis player needs to know all of these things, it works better if they can be learned holistically or impressionistically in order to get a clear mental image of what the flow of the stroke should feel like.

Similarly, when learning pronunciation, if a student is asked to think simultaneously about where to place the tongue, whether or not to use voicing, how to let the air flow, how to link words with preceding and following words, as well as what stress and intonation pattern to use, the complications become so great that the student cannot be expected to produce fluent, natural-sounding speech. A more productive approach is to help students form an acoustic impression of a short piece of language as a whole and learn it deeply, and only then to work toward understanding the specific elements that flow together to form it into English speech. This is the purpose of the Music of English tasks that appear throughout the Student's Book.

Pyramid tasks

Some units include a task in which students are asked to fill in the levels of the pronunciation pyramid. These tasks can help students gradually notice the key elements in a thought group, especially how the most important word is emphasized through making the strongest vowel the peak of information.

Quality Repetition helps students learn the rhythm, melody, and sounds of a new language.

Repetition is an old principle of language learning, but teachers quite naturally worry that many repetitions will lead to boredom. The fact is that boredom depends on how the repetition is done. Quality Repetition is based on a neurologically well-founded approach to learning the rhythm, melody, and sounds of language. Used primarily with Music of English activities, this approach depends both on highly varied encouragements to repeat a short chunk of language at fluent speed and on the psychological support of a choral setting. By repeating a short sentence or phrase in chorus, students learn the phrase "like a little song," fixing it in solid memory. Students reciting words or phrases alone tend to become uncertain and thus lose the rhythmic and melodic markers necessary to make the utterance clearly intelligible. Choral support, on the other hand, encourages each member of the group to stay exactly within the rhythmic structure.

The double purpose of this sort of practice is to give students personal possession of a fixed template of spoken English (which can later be used to analyze the core elements) and to provide a rising momentum of confidence for the class as a whole. This rising confidence outweighs any tendency to boredom because students are pleased to feel growing strength with each repetition.

The approach is explained in greater detail on page 6 of this Teacher's Resource and Assessment Book (Unit 1, Task J).

> We are what we repeatedly do –
> Excellence is not an act but a habit.
>
> > – Aristotle

Teaching and learning pronunciation can be rewarding experiences.

Many teachers think of pronunciation as a dauntingly technical subject, and they worry about looking professionally inadequate before their classes. This can lead them to teach in a way that emphasizes criticism, or it can lead them to try to teach too much, causing both teachers and students to lose confidence. The result is a common reluctance to teach pronunciation. In this Teacher's Resource and Assessment Book, I suggest several concepts and techniques to make the teaching of pronunciation a source of enjoyment and pride for both teacher and student.

Key to Sound Symbols

		Cambridge Dictionary of American English/ International Phonetic Alphabet	
Vowels			
Key words	*Clear Speech*		Your dictionary
cake, mail, pay	/eʸ/	/eɪ/	
pan, bat, hand	/æ/	/æ/	
tea, feet, key	/iʸ/	/iː/	
ten, well, red	/ɛ/	/e/	
ice, pie, night	/ɑʸ/	/ɑɪ/	
is, fish, will	/ɪ/	/ɪ/	
cone, road, know	/oʷ/	/oʊ/	
top, rock, stop	/ɑ/	/ɑ/	
blue, school, new, cube, few	/uʷ/	/uː/	
cut, cup, us, rust, love	/ʌ/	/ʌ/	
house, our, cow	/ɑʷ/	/ɑʊ/	
saw, talk, applause	/ɔ/	/ɔː/	
boy, coin, join	/ɔʸ/	/ɔɪ/	
put, book, woman	/ʊ/	/ʊ/	
alone, open, pencil, atom, ketchup	/ə/	/ə/	

Consonants			
Key words	*Clear Speech*	*Cambridge Dictionary of American English/* International Phonetic Alphabet	Your dictionary
bid, jo**b**	/**b**/	/b/	
do, fee**d**	/**d**/	/d/	
food, sa**f**e, lea**f**	/**f**/	/f/	
go, do**g**	/**g**/	/g/	
home, be**h**ind	/**h**/	/h/	
kiss, ba**ck**	/**k**/	/k/	
load, poo**l**, fai**l**	/**l**/	/l/	
man, plu**m**	/**m**/	/m/	
need, ope**n**	/**n**/	/n/	
sa**ng**, si**n**k	/**ŋ**/	/ŋ/	
pen, ho**p**e	/**p**/	/p/	
road, ca**r**d	/**r**/	/r/	
see, re**c**ent	/**s**/	/s/	
show, na**t**ion, wa**sh**	/**ʃ**/	/ʃ/	
team, mea**t**	/**t**/	/t/	
choose, wa**tch**	/**tʃ**/	/tʃ/	
think, bo**th**, tee**th**	/**θ**/	/θ/	
this, fa**th**er, tee**th**e	/**ð**/	/ð/	
visit, sa**v**e, lea**v**e	/**v**/	/v/	
watch, a**w**ay	/**w**/	/w/	
yes, on**i**on	/**y**/	/j/	
zoo, the**s**e, ea**s**e	/**z**/	/z/	
bei**g**e, mea**s**ure, A**s**ia	/**ʒ**/	/ʒ/	
jump, bri**dg**e	/**dʒ**/	/dʒ/	

1 Syllables

Unit overview

The *Clear Speech* Student's Book begins with the topic of syllable number because syllables are the basic building blocks of English rhythm, and **rhythm** may be the single most important element in clear English pronunciation. Every language has its own rhythm, and becoming familiar with that rhythm is a crucial part of learning a language.

When studying a new language, it is common for students to transfer the rhythm of their first language to the one they are learning. An English student whose first language is Spanish, for example, may speak English with Spanish rhythm. When English is practiced with the wrong rhythm, habits are formed that degrade intelligibility. The target sounds become more difficult to say accurately because the rhythm of the first language has a distorting effect on those sounds. When English is spoken with its correct rhythm, even difficult sounds become easier to say.

Learning the rhythm of English can even affect the efficiency of learning English grammar. Teachers sometimes notice, for example, that students with a good feel for English rhythm tend to have better control of small grammatical elements, such as articles or the past-tense **-ed** ending. These short, but important, elements are often missing from learners' speech as well as their writing. Students who are conscious of the rhythm patterns of English seem better able to notice them and produce them in their own speech.

Difficulties with syllables

In some languages, such as Chinese, each syllable tends to be conveyed by a single character, so when reading there is no confusion about the number of syllables in a given word. In English, however, interpreting the written language is not always so easy. For example, the word "Wednesday" is said with two syllables, but it looks like three.

Each language also has its own rules for the composition of syllables. For instance, some languages do not allow two or more consonants to be pronounced together, but many English words contain consonant clusters. Learners whose first language does not allow for such clusters tend to separate the consonants by adding a vowel between them. This creates a new syllable and may make it difficult for students to distinguish certain pairs of words (e.g., "train / terrain," "blow / below," "broke / baroque"). The rules of the first language may cause students to add syllables for other reasons (e.g., "eschool" for "school"). Other students will systematically drop syllables that are difficult for them to hear or pronounce (e.g., /ˈgoʷ•mʌnt/ for the word "government"). Adding or dropping syllables in these ways interferes with intelligibility.

Note: The ' in "government" above means that the following syllable is stressed. The • means a syllable separation.

> **Teaching tip** The table on the next page shows some cross-language comparisons of syllable numbers that you can use for an entertaining discovery activity. These words are *loan words*, pronounced similarly in several languages but often with different numbers of syllables. This type of comparison works especially well for a class composed of students from various language backgrounds. It will encourage them to recognize familiar words in a new way. If your students all share the same first language, then they may be most interested in words shared by that language and English. Choose the examples that fit your class best, and encourage students to add any other loan words they can think of to the lists.
>
> *Note:* English uses fewer syllables because it has so many consonant clusters. Many other languages tend to require a vowel in between the consonants, making more syllables. Your students may spell these words differently or count the syllables differently, but still use more syllables than English. Japanese double vowels can be counted either as extra long or as two syllables.

English	Spanish	Japanese	Mandarin	Portuguese (Brazil)	Korean	German
□□ chocolate	□□□□ chocolate	□□□□□ chokoreeto	□□□ quiaokeli	□□□□ chocolate	□□□ choccoret	□□□□ Schokolade
□ click		□□□ kurikku		□□ clique	□□ keullik	□ Klick
□□ e-mail		□□□□□ iimeeru	□□□ yimeier	□□□ email	□□□ yimeil	□□ E-Mail
□□ service	□□□□ servicio	□□□□ saabisu		□□□ serviço	□□□ seobiseu	□□ Service
□□□ hamburger	□□□□ hamburguesa	□□□□□ hanbaagaa	□□□ hanbao	□□□ hambúrguer	□□□ haembeogeo	□□□ Hamburger
□ school	□□□ escuela	□□□□ sukuuru		□□□ escola	□□ seukul	□□ Schule
□□ address		□□□ adoresu		□□□□ endereço	□□□□ eodeureseu	□□□ Adresse
□ cheese	□□ queso	□□□ chiisu	□□ qisi	□□ queijo	□□ chijeu	□□ Käse
□ cream	□□ crema	□□□□ kuriimu	□□□ kelinmu	□□ creme	□□ keurim	□□ □ Kreme / Krem
□□ ice cream		□□□□□□□ aisukuriimu			□□□□□ aiseukeulim	□□□ □□ Eiskreme / Eiskrem
□ milk		□□□ miruku			□□ milkeu	□ Milch
□ class	□□ clase	□□□ kurasu		□ classe	□□□ keullaseu	□□ Klasse
□ bus		□□ basu	□□ bashi		□□ beoseo	

Unfamiliar vocabulary

Because students like to know the meaning of the words they are saying, they are likely to be more satisfied with an exercise if you quickly define any of the words that are new to them. However, discussion of vocabulary can absorb too much valuable class time, and your main objective should always be to keep class attention focused on pronunciation. For this reason, it is usually best to assign unknown words as dictionary work for outside of class. Students can look up the words at home and bring the definitions to class. This will provide an automatic occasion for review of the teaching point when the class goes over the definitions.

Most dictionaries give not only the meaning of words but their syllabification. Good preparation for this type of homework assignment is to show students how syllables are marked in their dictionaries. If students are using different dictionaries, then direct them to study how to tap out the markings in their particular dictionaries. If time is available, the different systems for marking syllables could be discussed in class. In any event, students need to learn how to use their dictionaries as a resource for understanding syllabification and word stress.

⌒ A Introducing syllables
Class CD 1, Track 2

First, play the audio or read the lists of words in horizontal order. Then, for an additional challenge, read the words in random order and ask the students to identify the word.

> **Teaching tip**   It is helpful to have students tap their hands or feet to count the syllables. Then call on individuals and ask how many syllables are in a given word. Another possibility is to have the class hold up their fingers to indicate the number of syllables in each word. With this method, it is possible to check the entire class at a glance.

⌒ B Tapping the syllables
Class CD 1, Track 3

Students from different language backgrounds experience different types of difficulty with syllables. For instance, Japanese automatically devoices high vowels (as in "eat" and "boot") between voiceless consonants or following a voiceless consonant at the end of a word. Therefore, the Japanese pronunciation of a name like "Setsuko" or "Hiroshi" is apt to sound like two syllables to an English-speaking listener. On the other hand, Korean students may tend to add vowels at the end of words that end in a sibilant, such as "fish" or "mess."

Another problem for Japanese students is that they may count nasal sounds (/n/, /m/, and /g/) as syllables, with the result that a word like "instant" can sound like a five- or even six-syllable word to a Japanese speaker. To deal with this problem, you can explain that an English syllable usually needs a vowel sound in the center. However, the most effective solution to this and other syllable-related problems is to use tapping while listening until students intuitively perceive syllables in an English sense.

> **Teaching tip**   Some students are reluctant to tap the table to demonstrate the number of syllables. Although some kind of physical marking is needed to truly develop a sense of syllable rhythm, there are various ways to remove any embarrassment from the activity. Students can tap a pencil or, for more privacy, tap their knees under the desk. Another option is to have them touch thumb to finger to mark the syllable beat. If they touch a different finger for each syllable, this will also help them count the number of syllables in a particular word or sentence.

If a student resists even this hidden motion, it may be that there is a fundamental undercurrent of resistance to changing rhythm. Students sometimes have psychological barriers to "sounding foreign," and this makes them resist unconsciously. Pronunciation is far more apt to activate this kind of reluctance than drilling in more psychologically neutral aspects of language like grammar or vocabulary. After all, we learn the rhythm of our native language long before we learn to say words, and it is part of our sense of who we are and where we belong. For this reason, it is wise to notice resistance and not to meet it head on, but to gradually coax the students along to the new rhythm. If limericks and other related activities are amusing and relaxing, these can go a long way toward helping lower the *affective filter* of unconscious resistance.

C Which word is different?

Class CD 1, Track 4

Listening tasks are a good introduction to new concepts or new sounds. This particular task helps students distinguish between words with different numbers of syllables. Despite what would appear to be a worrisome variety of reasons for English learners not to get the point right away, most students do pick up the idea of syllables rapidly. The concept is repeated regularly in the units that follow.

Note: The ' in the audio script below means that the following syllable is stressed. The • means a syllable separation.

Audio Script

1. fish, fish, fishy
   /fɪʃ/, /fɪʃ/, /ˈfɪ•ʃiʸ/
2. care, care, careful
   /kær/, /kær/, /ˈkær•fəl/
3. can't, cannot, can't
   /kænt/, /kæ'nɑt/, /kænt/
4. state, estate, estate
   /steʸt/, /ɪ'steʸt/, /ɪ'steʸt/
5. sport, support, sport
   /spɔrt/, /sə'pɔrt/, /spɔrt/
6. sit, sit, city
   /sɪt/, /sɪt/, /ˈsɪ•tiʸ/
7. cracked, cracked, correct
   /krækt/, /krækt/, /kə'rɛkt/
8. dish, dishes, dishes
   /dɪʃ/, /ˈdɪ•ʃəz/, /ˈdɪ•ʃəz/

Answer Key

	X	Y	Z
1.			✓
2.			✓
3.		✓	
4.	✓		
5.		✓	
6.			✓
7.			✓
8.	✓		

D Which word do you hear?

Class CD 1, Track 5

This is another listening task, but more difficult than Task C.

> **Teaching tip** After students have listened and circled the words, you may direct them to practice saying the words they circled.

Audio Script

1. messy   /ˈmɛ•siʸ/
2. below   /bə'loʷ/
3. parade   /pə'reʸd/
4. loud   /lɑʷd/
5. support   /sə'pɔrt/
6. round   /rɑʷnd/
7. claps   /klæps/
8. closed   /kloʷzd/
9. state   /steʸt/
10. excuse   /ɛk'skyuʷz/

Answer Key

1. mess   (messy)
2. blow   (below)
3. prayed   (parade)
4. (loud)   aloud
5. sport   (support)
6. (round)   around
7. (claps)   collapse
8. (closed)   closet
9. (state)   estate
10. squeeze   (excuse)

E Pair work: One or two syllables?

Pair work tasks give every student the chance to practice speaking and listening at the same time, and this makes more efficient use of class time than individual recitation. It also means that students are focusing on each other and on intelligibility, rather than suffering the negative tension of solo recitation. This reinforces the idea that all the students are working together toward reasonable goals.

The main advantage of pair challenges like this one is that they demonstrate the practical usefulness of speaking clearly. Student B's answer depends on Student A's initial remark, so Student A must be sure to produce the target sound or target rhythmic pattern clearly in order to trigger the correct response from Student B.

Pair work activities like this one can be conducted in different ways. In general, the following procedures have been most effective:

- Give students the opportunity to read the words first before actually beginning the challenge with their partners.
- To introduce the concept of pair work, read a word from the task, and have students supply the appropriate response. Going through the whole set of items this way is especially helpful for lower-level classes. More advanced students will not need such preparation before they perform the task on their own.
- Partners should switch roles as Student A and Student B. They could flip a coin to decide who will be Student A first, then go through the whole set, switching roles once they have finished.
- Remind students not to consistently choose the first or the second word, but to make this a real challenge for the listener by making their choices less predictable.
- Partners should be changed from time to time to add variety to the listening challenge. Learning to accommodate to different voices is valuable training. This works even better if the students have different first languages.
- Walk around and listen while students do the task. It may work best not to correct mistakes on the spot but to take notes and give feedback to the whole class at the end of the exercise. This keeps the students' attention focused on their responsibility to listen to each other.
- Pair work can be made harder by asking the listeners to cover up the words. Pair work tasks can also be used as a quiz for the class.

Pair work activities should take about 10 minutes, but class speed varies a great deal. In general, you should halt the exercise when a majority of the pairs have finished going through the list of challenges. If there is a general eagerness to continue by running through the challenges again, you can give an extension of time. On the other hand, if the exercise is too easy for your students, it is best to cut the number of items in half or eliminate the activity entirely.

F Extra syllable in past tense verbs
Class CD 1, Track 6

Some students may speak languages that do not normally allow a consonant at the end of a word (e.g., some East and Southeast Asian languages). They may feel you are simply being fussy by reminding them to pay attention to final consonants that they are likely not to notice. This particular task can motivate students to sharpen their final consonants by making clear the grammatical significance of these sounds.

Answer Key

fainted (2)	landed (2)	worked (1)
laughed (1)	added (2)	folded (2)
started (2)	watched (1)	closed (1)
caused (1)	planned (1)	
treated (2)	counted (2)	
asked (1)	cooked (1)	

G Counting syllables in past tense verbs
Class CD 1, Track 7

Audio Script

1. paint /ˈpeʸnt/   painted /ˈpeʸn•təd/
2. clean /kliʸn/   cleaned /kliʸnd/
3. need /niʸd/   needed /ˈniʸ•dəd/
4. decide /dəˈsɑʸd/   decided /dəˈsɑʸ•dəd/
5. dislike /dɪsˈlɑʸk/   disliked /dɪsˈlɑʸkt/
6. prepare /prəˈpær/   prepared /prəˈpærd/
7. represent /rɛ•prəˈzɛnt/   represented /rɛ•prəˈzɛn•təd/
8. entertain /ɛn•tərˈteʸn/   entertained /ɛn•tərˈteʸnd/

Answer Key

1. painted (2)
2. cleaned (1)
3. needed (2)
4. decided (3)
5. disliked (2)
6. prepared (2)
7. represented (4)
8. entertained (3)

H Pair work: Past or present?

If your students are enrolled in a full English program, this task will reinforce the grammar lessons they are getting in other classes. If pronunciation is their only subject (in a workplace class, for instance), they may initially find focusing on grammar to be difficult. In either case, the purpose of this exercise is to remind students in a practical way that syllable number affects the meaning of a word.

🎧 I Silent letters
Class CD 1, Track 8

There are regional variations in the syllable number of some of these words, but the following answer key reflects the most common pronunciations.

Answer Key

□	□□	□□□	□□□□
walke̶d	busi̶ness	vege̶table	labo̶ratory
planne̶d	Wed̶ne̶sday	inte̶resting	eleme̶ntary
close̶d	eve̶ry	diffe̶rently	
talke̶d	fami̶ly		

> **Teaching tip** Silent letters are puzzling to students who have learned English through reading. A graphic way to focus attention on the silence of these letters is to use the *vanishing letters* technique.
>
> Make a poster listing words with silent vowel letters (e.g., "evening," "filled," "lonely"), but write the silent letters with a yellow marker. (Any color can be used for the other letters.) Show this poster and then cover it with a red acetate screen. You can use half of a red plastic report cover for a screen. The yellow letters will disappear behind the red screen. Each silent letter will occupy a space invisibly, as a visual reminder not to say it.

🎧 J Music of English
Class CD 1, Track 9

This Music of English box teaches students rhythm and intonation patterns for questions and answers about the meanings of words. They will use the melodic patterns they learn in the pair work task that follows.

Music of English tasks help students master a short sequence of English syllables in the same way that they would learn a little song. Through the technique called *Quality Repetition*, they can deeply memorize the melody and timing of this short stream of spoken language. Once they have come to "own" the little piece of English, they can analyze its specific elements.

Music of English tasks can be conducted in the following way:

Either play the audio or read the sentences in the Music of English box several times at a near-native, normal speed. Then direct students, as a class, to say the sentences along with you. It is up to you to determine how many times students should repeat the lines chorally. The more they repeat them, the more securely the music will be imprinted in their memory. Keep in mind that, while you may get bored with the recurring sentences, students do not get bored because they feel themselves growing more confident with each repetition.

The rationale behind the technique outlined above has been set forth in the following quote by Olle Kjellin, MD, PhD, who uses this approach to teach Swedish pronunciation:

> [Through the process of choral repetition,] not only is the student learning to internalize all the elements which make the rhythm interrelate (reduction, elongation, linking, etc.), but the melody is being fixed to the sentence. So if the student repeats many, many times along at the same time with other voices giving support, there is a good chance of mastering the whole music of the piece. People often can learn to pronounce perfectly when they are singing a foreign song they like, and these chunks of language are like little songs.
>
> Keep in mind that the traditional "Repeat after me" tends to encourage slowing down and concentration on the individual sounds (**segmentals**), whereas simultaneous repetition tends to encourage students to focus on the rhythm and melody (**suprasegmentals**). Listeners are less likely to notice individual sound errors if the musical patterns are correct.
>
> Teachers naturally assume that slowing the rate of their speech model will help the students. But this tends to overload the listener's working memory. Most people can only remember for one or two seconds, especially when they are listening to a language with which they are not thoroughly familiar. Speech that is too slow is actually harder to follow. Of course sometimes it is helpful to slow down a specific example so that students can notice a particular part of it. But for repetition practice, it is better to teach the phrase or short sentence at or near native, normal speed.

(Kjellin, personal correspondence, 1999)

This particular Music of English box helps students learn the rhythm and intonation patterns for questions and answers about spelling. The students will then use the melody they learn to ask and answer questions in Task K.

Note: Alternative pitch patterns are possible for almost all English sentences, but the Music of English boxes present patterns that are most common.

> **Teaching tip** Following the pitch line with your hand is a good kinesthetic reinforcement of an intonation pattern. With your hand, model the rise and fall of the pitch as you say the sentences or as the audio plays, and have students do this with you several times. This method can be used for each Music of English box in the Student's Book.

K Pair work: Asking about spelling

Spelling out loud (saying the names of the letters) is an important skill for students who have trouble being understood. That is why practicing these questions and answers is so important. Questions like these will be used in exercises throughout the Student's Book.

> **Teaching tip** When spelling out loud, each letter is like a separate syllable, and the pitch usually rises and falls on the last syllable to indicate that the series of letters is finished. To model this, write several words on the board. Spell each word with a rise / fall intonation on the last letter, and have students repeat it with you. This will match the pitch line in the Music of English box in Task J.

L Music of English
Class CD 1, Track 10

The skill being practiced here is the use of contrastive pitch patterns between two different words, "easy" and "hard." This contrast helps focus attention on the main point of the question and the answer. It is preparation for Task M.

N Check yourself: Counting syllables
Class CD 1, Track 11

"Check yourself" tasks give students the opportunity to assess their own progress.

Note that the words "this is" (in the first sentence) may cause overcorrection, with too much emphasis on the word "is," which should normally be de-emphasized. Such overcorrection is justified at this point because of the importance of getting students to feel the presence of each syllable. No matter how unstressed or short a syllable is, it still must be present.

Answer Key

This is the <u>first</u> <u>city</u> they <u>visited</u> when they <u>traveled</u> here on <u>business</u>.

They were so <u>pleased</u> that they <u>decided</u> to stay <u>seven</u> extra days.

O Syllable number game

Games are valuable in a pronunciation class because they lower tension. Allow five to ten minutes for teams to make their lists and five minutes for them to put the lists on the board and assign points. Here are some additional words to suggest if your students get stuck:

One syllable: milk, bread, peas, beef, cheese
Two syllables: chicken, butter, carrot, lettuce
Three syllables: potato, spaghetti, cucumber
Four syllables: avocado, enchilada

One syllable: Spain, Greece, Chad
Two syllables: Norway, Denmark, Egypt
Three syllables: Singapore, Morocco, Germany, Italy
Four syllables: Argentina, Venezuela, Mauritania

P Dictation: How many syllables?
Class CD 1, Track 12

Dictation is a valuable tool. Both student and teacher may be surprised by how many simple words are not heard well, even by advanced students.

If you do not have the audio or prefer to read the sentences out loud to the class, you might want to consider the following: Some teachers are strict about reading the sentences only once, no matter how often students ask for another reading. The theory behind this approach is to make students learn to pay close attention. Of course, how you read the sentences depends on how you judge the ability of your students to process what you are saying.

It is important at any level that you do not dictate the sentences one word at a time (e.g, "They . . . walked . . . to . . . the . . . store . . . to . . . buy . . . chocolate."). Instead, break the sentences up into thought groups (e.g., "They walked to the store / to buy chocolate."). If the dictation sentences seem too easy, increase the challenge by reading them without long pauses between the thought groups. Another way to increase the challenge is to read more quickly and with more reduction of small words like "to" and "the."

If the dictation sentences are too difficult for your students, create simpler sentences. For example, the sentences in this dictation task can be replaced by simpler ones containing past tense verbs and other words that may cause syllable number difficulty.

If students have access to the class audio, this task can be done as homework. They can then turn in the dictated sentences for correction. When correcting this particular dictation task, however, keep in mind that spelling errors are not important at this point; what is important is the students' awareness of syllable number.

> **Teaching tip**   One useful approach is to have students take dictation on the board. This will help them recognize their errors. Another good approach is to have students dictate to each other, as this emphasizes both speaking and listening and fosters a collaborative atmosphere. Students also will find that it is easier to notice their partners' mistakes than it is for them to notice their own.

Answer Key

1. He works in an interesting business. (9)
2. They walked to the store to buy chocolate. (9)
3. Vegetables are expensive right now. (9)
4. We recorded everything and waited for the results. (14)
5. I opened the closet and laughed at what I saw. (12)

Unit 1 Quiz is available on page 76.

2 Vowels and Vowel Rules

Unit overview

English learners benefit in many ways from learning how to guess the pronunciation of words they encounter in written form. It is an essential skill that enables them to use printed material to read out loud on their own and practice what they have been taught in class. But when students guess the pronunciation of a printed word incorrectly and then make that word part of their active vocabulary, the mispronunciation tends to become fossilized and difficult to correct later on.

This unit introduces 10 basic vowel sounds as well as two rules that will help students guess the pronunciation of many common vowel spellings. These "decoding" rules (the One Vowel Rule and the Two Vowel Rule) are based on phonics rules traditionally used to teach native English-speaking children to read. Unfortunately, the traditional form of these rules tend not to work as well for people who are not native English speakers. This is because their mental inventories of sounds and their writing systems may be quite different. Even if their first language uses the same alphabet, the letters may have different "names" (e.g., the vowel letters, or the consonant letters -j- and -g-).

A further problem with traditional phonics rules is that the examples given to support them are almost always monosyllabic words (e.g., "bit," "bite," "boat"), but the adult ESL / EFL student needs to decode multi-syllabic words, too.

Since traditional phonics rules are not completely suitable for the ESL / EFL classroom, the vowel rules given in this book have been written specifically for ESL / EFL students. They are based on the spellings-to-sound findings of a major corpus-based study (Carney, 1994) and are presented in Tasks G and K of this unit. See the charts on page 144 of Appendix C in the Student's Book to find out how often the vowel rules work. The purpose of giving these percentages of time that the rules work is to convince students that learning them is worth the effort.

A Introducing vowels

Most of the vowel sounds in English can be divided into two basic categories such as the contrast between the vowel sounds in the words "mate" and "mat." Spelling books have traditionally described these two types of vowels as *long vowels* and *short vowels*, respectively. While this terminology is often used to teach reading

to native speakers of English, it tends to confuse ESL students when they also have to learn to use the same terms, *long* and *short*, for the contrast in length so essential for English stress (Unit 3). Leading experts in the field of ESL / EFL pronunciation reserve these terms to describe actual sound duration (Dauer, 1993; Gilbert, 2001; Grant, 2010; Miller, 2000; Morley, 1992). For this reason, *Clear Speech* does not use the terms *long* and *short* to refer to these contrasting vowel categories. Instead, the terms *alphabet vowel sound* and *relative vowel sound* are used. The rationale for the use of these terms will become clear as you and your students work through the tasks in this unit.

In the following tasks, students will learn and practice the five alphabet vowel sounds and the five relative vowel sounds. Other vowel sounds, including schwa (/ə/), will be introduced in later units, once the 10 basic sounds have been firmly grasped.

B Alphabet vowel sounds
Class CD 1, Track 13

The alphabet vowel sounds are presented first because they are a natural part of presenting the alphabet. Furthermore, they are closer to the vowel sounds used in most languages and are, therefore, more likely to be easier for students.

For most students, the new concept presented here is the *off-glide*, the small sound change that takes place at the end of each alphabet vowel sound. This small change in sound is caused by an upward shift of the tongue and a change in the position of the lips – and both of these movements take place when the alphabet vowel sounds are being spoken.

C The tongue in alphabet vowel sounds
Class CD 1, Track 14

This task focuses students' attention on the upward shift of the tongue that takes place when pronouncing an alphabet vowel sound. The alphabet vowel sounds are represented here (and throughout the Student's Book) by the phonetic symbols /eʸ/, /iʸ/, /ɑʸ/, /oʷ/, and /uʷ/. Each symbol contains a superscript /ʸ/ or /ʷ/, which serves to indicate the presence of an off-glide.

Note: The letter -u- is usually pronounced as in "blue" /bluʷ/, but less often it is pronounced like the alphabet sound with a little /ʸ/ on-glide, as in "cube" /kyuʷb/.

D The lips in alphabet vowel sounds
Class CD 1, Track 15

This task focuses students' attention on how the lips change shape when pronouncing an alphabet vowel sound. The superscript /^{y}/ for the front vowel sounds /e^y/, /i^y/, and /ɑ^y/ should help students notice the need for a shift of the tongue and a spreading of the lips. The superscript /^{w}/ for the back vowels /o^w/ and /u^w/ should serve to remind students to round their lips at the end of these sounds.

E Listening to alphabet vowel sounds
Class CD 1, Track 16

Research suggests that, unlike consonants, vowel sounds are initially learned best through listening tasks, not through repeating out loud (Fucci, D. et al., 1977). The problem with having students say the words out loud too soon is that they are likely to give themselves a misleading acoustic image. This acoustic image that they hear themselves saying is then likely to become fossilized as a fixed habit of speaking. For this reason, it is better to begin vowel study with tasks that give students the opportunity to listen without having to produce the sounds.

Students should also be given plenty of opportunity to practice new sounds silently or by whispering. Doing so helps them concentrate on how their mouths feel before they actually speak out loud. Furthermore, because whispering is so quiet, it saves the students from any embarrassment they might feel when making those tentative first efforts.

The key words for the alphabet vowel sounds are "cake," "tea," "ice," "cone," and "blue." Frequent review of these words will give students a resource to refer back to when they are puzzled by a new word.

F Which word has the same alphabet vowel sound?
Class CD 1, Track 17

Audio Script

1. tea	eat, ate
/ti^y/	/i^{y}t/, /e^{y}t/
2. ice	place, rice
/ɑ^{y}s/	/ple^{y}s/, /rɑ^{y}s/
3. blue	suit, so
/blu^w/	/su^{w}t/, /so^w/
4. cone	coat, cute
/ko^{w}n/	/ko^{w}t/, /kyu^{w}t/
5. cake	name, time
/ke^{y}k/	/ne^{y}m/, /tɑ^{y}m/

Answer Key

1. tea	(eat) ate
2. ice	place, (rice)
3. blue	(suit) so
4. cone	(coat) cute
5. cake	(name) time

G The Two Vowel Rule for alphabet vowel sounds

In the preceding tasks, students learned to identify the alphabet vowel sounds when they hear them. In Task G, students learn a rule that will help them know when a vowel letter should be pronounced with its alphabet vowel sound. The Two Vowel Rule enables students to decode two types of one-syllable word: those that contain two vowel letters side by side (e.g., "soap," "steam") and those that contain a vowel letter followed by a consonant and a silent -e- (e.g., "hope," "late"). In order to use the rule, students must, of course, be familiar with the alphabet vowel sounds presented earlier.

> **Teaching tip** At this point, it is a good idea to have students read over the word lists in Task E in order for them to see how the Two Vowel Rule can be used to guess the pronunciation of the vowels in each word.

H Practicing alphabet vowel sounds
Class CD 1, Track 18

After listening and repeating the words with the audio, you could put the words on the board. Then point to the words in random order, and have students say the words.

I Relative vowel sounds
Class CD 1, Track 19

The term *relative vowel* means a sound related to the *alphabet vowel*. Unlike the alphabet vowel sounds, the relative vowel sounds (/æ/, /ɛ/, /ɪ/, /ɑ/, and /ʌ/) do not have off-glides. They happen to be the most common pronunciations of the English vowel letters, but they are more challenging to learn because they are typically foreign to many English learners. In fact, relatively few languages have the vowels /æ/, as in "pan," or /ɪ/, as in "is." Memorizing the key words for the relative vowel sounds ("pan," "ten," "is," "top," and "cut") will help students remember the five sounds.

🎧 J Which word is different?
Class CD 1, Track 20

Audio Script

1. aid, add, aid
   /eʸd/, /æd/, /eʸd/
2. these, this, these
   /ðiʸz/, /ðɪs/, /ðiʸz/
3. lease, lease, less
   /liʸs/, /liʸs/, /lɛs/
4. bead, bead, bed
   /biʸd/, /biʸd/, /bɛd/
5. tile, tile, till
   /taʸl/, /taʸl/, /tɪl/
6. pine, pin, pine
   /paʸn/, /pɪn/, /paʸn/
7. chess, cheese, cheese
   /tʃɛs/, /tʃiʸz/, /tʃiʸz/
8. bite, bite, bit
   /baʸt/, /baʸt/, /bɪt/

Answer Key

	X	Y	Z
1.		✓	
2.		✓	
3.			✓
4.			✓
5.			✓
6.		✓	
7.	✓		
8.			✓

K The One Vowel Rule for relative vowel sounds

> **Teaching tip** Make two columns on the board labeled "Alphabet Vowel Sounds" and "Relative Vowel Sounds." Direct students to form teams, and have them compete to find words for each column. The team that comes up with the most words in five minutes wins.

🎧 L Practicing relative vowel sounds
Class CD 1, Track 21

After listening and repeating the words with the audio, you could put the words on the board. Then point to the words in random order, and have students say the words.

🎧 M Contrasting alphabet vowel sounds and relative vowel sounds
Class CD 1, Track 22

Ask for volunteers to give the Two Vowel Rule and the One Vowel Rule, to remind the whole class before working through Task M.

🎧 N Guessing the pronunciation of a word
Class CD 1, Track 23

From this point on, students should be encouraged to guess the pronunciation of new words they encounter by using the One Vowel Rule and the Two Vowel Rule. In Unit 3, they will be learning about stress. A stressed syllable tends to fit the Vowel Rules, so students eventually will be able to guess at multi-syllabic words, too. While these rules do not always work, they do work often enough to give students a rising momentum of confidence when attempting to pronounce new words. (See the charts on page 144 in Appendix C of the Student's Book to find out how often the Vowel Rules are likely to work.)

Audio Script

1. rove   /roʷv/
2. span   /spæn/
3. vice   /vaʸs/
4. moat   /moʷt/
5. slain   /sleʸn/
6. meld   /mɛld/
7. stint   /stɪnt/
8. jute   /dʒuʷt/

Answer Key

	Alphabet vowel sound	Relative vowel sound
1.	✓	
2.		✓
3.	✓	
4.	✓	
5.	✓	
6.		✓
7.		✓
8.	✓	

O Listening to contrasting vowels in sentences
Class CD 1, Track 24

Audio Script

1. Did you say "hope"?
2. How do you spell "less"?
3. What does "tap" mean?
4. I need a pen.
5. Did you want this?
6. Do you like chess?

Answer Key

1. Did you say "hope" / "hop"?
2. How do you spell "lease" / "less"?
3. What does "tape" / "tap" mean?
4. I need a pan / pen.
5. Did you want this / these?
6. Do you like chess / cheese?

P Music of English
Class CD 1, Track 25

It is important for students to learn how to verify information when they are not sure what was just said. This Music of English box teaches the musical patterns associated with the questions and answers that students will use to verify information in Task Q.

R Pair work: Contrasting vowels in sentences

The patterns for the questions and answers in this pair-work practice were taught in Unit 1, Task L, on page 7 of the Student's Book.

S Check yourself: Alphabet vowel sounds and relative vowel sounds
Class CD 1, Track 26

> **Teaching tip** At this point, it would be a good idea to ask students to start bringing in new one-syllable words they have learned outside of class. They can then analyze these words as a group to see which vowel category the words might belong to. This kind of analytical practice should be reinforced often so that it becomes an automatic way to think about any new vocabulary items students encounter.

T Dictation
Class CD 1, Track 27

Answer Key

1. Did you say "teen" or "ten"?
2. Is it a big pine?
3. I hope I can see it.
4. Chocolate is not a vegetable.
5. Several elementary schools opened late.

U Using the vowel symbols

This first task using one of the levels of the pronunciation pyramid is an important way not only to review the vowel symbols but to remind students of how the peak vowels – the vowel in the primary stressed syllable of the focus word – fit into the system of spoken English. The peak vowel indicates the peak of communication, so it goes in the peak level of the pronunciation pyramid.

Students are asked to copy the sound symbols because drawing something is a different way of thinking about it. These symbols are specific to the sound, and provide a more secure way of understanding it than simply looking at the letters in the spelling. Once students get used to drawing the symbols, they can use them later to help remember how a new word is pronounced.

Answer Key

1.	is	/ɪ/
2.	ten	/ɛ/
3.	blue	/uʷ/
4.	cut	/ʌ/
5.	ice	/aʸ/

Unit 2 Quiz is available on page 77.

3 Word Stress and Vowel Length

Unit overview

Students tend to think that word stress is some sort of added decoration, or else they do not notice it at all. But far from being merely decorative, stress is an essential part of the pronunciation of English words. This is because native English speakers tend to keep a mental store of vocabulary according to stress patterns (Brown, 1977, 1990; Levelt, 1989). When a word is said with an incorrect stress pattern, the native English-speaking listener may spend time searching for the word in the wrong stress category. By the time the listener realizes something is wrong, the original sequence of sounds may have been forgotten. A stress pattern mistake can, therefore, cause a great deal of confusion, especially if it is accompanied by any other kind of error.

Errors in word stress are often the result of transfer from a learner's first language. For example, stress in Korean, Punjabi, or Czech usually falls on the first syllable of a word, whereas stress in Hebrew usually falls on the last syllable. In English, stress can be on any syllable. (Some stress patterns are more common than others in English, as students will learn in Unit 5.)

The following scene illustrates the kind of confusion that can result from mistakes in word stress. This exchange actually took place in the United States when a Japanese visitor tried to make a small purchase at an electronic supply store. The visitor needed a resistor for an electronic gadget, so he asked the clerk for a "**reg**ista." The clerk, however, could not understand what he wanted. The customer, recognizing that there was something wrong with his pronunciation, tried different ways to clarify.

Customer: **Reg**ista?
Clerk: *(looking at the cash register)* Excuse me?
Customer: *(trying a change of vowel)* **Rah**gista?
Clerk: Sir?
Customer: *(deciding the problem was the /**dʒ**/ sound)* **Rah**zista!
Clerk: *(impatiently)* I'm sorry, we don't have anything like that.
Customer: *(furious)* Right here! Look at this picture! A **rah**zista!
Clerk: *(suddenly understanding)* Oh, you mean a re**sis**tor!

The above incident illustrates how errors in word stress can create serious barriers to intelligibility, even when the individual sounds in a word are pronounced correctly or nearly correctly. The story also shows how a learner can keep making changes until finally figuring out the problem.

Signals of word stress

It has long been common practice to teach stress as if it were synonymous with loudness, but this approach is not the most useful. The two most powerful signals for indicating a stressed syllable in English are:

1. Vowel length
2. Vowel clarity

Musical signals, such as vowel lengthening and pitch change, are used in most languages, but they are not always used for the same functions or in the same combinations as they are in English. For this reason, it is important to teach students the special ways that English uses these musical elements.

This unit focuses students' attention on the first element mentioned above: vowel length. It is the signal for word stress that most students find easiest to control (Chela de Rodriguez, 1991). Vowel clarity will be dealt with in Unit 4. There is another important musical signal, pitch change, but *Clear Speech* reserves this feature for the signaling of sentence-level emphasis, not for word stress (see Units 6 through 9). It is true, nevertheless, that a word, when said alone, does have a pitch pattern that helps indicate which syllable is stressed. Consider the following pair of words, for example:

atom   atomic

For "atom," the pitch starts out high and then drops. For "atomic," the pitch rises on the second syllable and then drops on the third. These pitch changes occur in single words when they are said in isolation because a single word is, in effect, a complete remark. However, when these words are spoken as part of a sentence, the pitch changes will not actually be noticeable unless the words have particular significance in that sentence (Bolinger, 1986; Fry, 1955). (See Unit 6 for more on this.)

Degrees of vowel length

In many languages, syllables tend to be roughly equal in length. But clarity in spoken English depends on the variable length of the syllables. In English, the vowel sound at the center of a syllable may have three basic lengths: *stressed*, *unstressed*, or *reduced*. These three degrees of length are highlighted below in the example word "economic."

1. Stressed:
   The third vowel in "econ**o**mic"
   (Referred to in some books as *primary stress*)
2. Unstressed:
   The first vowel sound in "**e**conomic"
   (Referred to in some books as *secondary stress*)
3. Reduced:
   The second and fourth vowel sounds in "economic"
   (The schwa sound, presented in Unit 4)

These vowel lengths are not exact measurements, so there is no point in trying to reduce English to musical notation or asking students to practice three-way timing contrasts. Your aim should simply be, at this point, to increase students' awareness of the irregularity of English syllable length and the general principle that "length adds strength."

The first priority for learning English stress is the ability to make and hear a clear contrast between stressed and reduced vowels. For this reason, the second level of stress – the unstressed, but not reduced, vowel – will not be discussed until Unit 4.

A Stressed syllables
Class CD 1, Track 28

The word "banana" was selected for this task because it contains examples of both stressed and reduced vowel sounds, all represented by the same letter (-a-). The pyramid gives a visual image of which syllable has the peak vowel, and the picture of the hands stretching a rubber band gives another way to experience the lengthening needed for the stressed syllable.

> Teaching tip   Stretching wide, heavy rubber bands while practicing the lengthened vowel in "banana" and in other words can provide students with a kinesthetic exercise to reinforce the short / long contrast needed to call attention to the stressed syllable. The use of rubber bands is especially helpful for students whose own language rhythm is based mainly on the equal length of syllables (e.g., Spanish, Japanese, and many other languages). Thin bands are apt to break and also do not give the full impression of the effort involved in making some syllables longer than others.

C Listening for vowel length
Class CD 1, Track 29

Note: Do not worry about what is exactly included when students underline a syllable as long as it has the correct vowel in its center.

Answer Key

sofa	attract	solution	going
oven	event	arrangement	horrible
action	arrange	pollution	energy
London	Brazil	Atlanta	Ottawa
England	Berlin	Alberta	Washington

D Saying stressed syllables
Class CD 1, Track 30

Point out to students that the syllable squares first used in Unit 1 of the Student's Book are being used in this task in a modified form. A syllable rectangle is used here to indicate a stressed syllable.

E Saying words with more than two syllables
Class CD 1, Track 31

> Teaching tip   This is another opportunity to direct students to use rubber bands to indicate vowel length while they repeat the words. After this point, you can just display a rubber band as a visual reminder to pay attention to length, especially if a stress error has just occurred.

F Pair work: Stress in acronyms
Class CD 1, Track 32

If needed, review the pattern for stress in a series of letters as practiced in Music of English in Unit 1, Task J, on page 6.

G The Two Vowel Rule with multi-syllable words
Class CD 1, Track 33

This task offers an opportunity for students to review the Two Vowel Rule learned in Unit 2 and to apply the rule to the longer words they are now working with. Remind students about the extra length needed in the stressed syllable of each word.

H The One Vowel Rule with multi-syllable words
Class CD 1, Track 34

Here the One Vowel Rule is applied to words with two and three syllables. Remind students to use an extra long vowel sound for stressed syllables.

> **Teaching tip** Make two columns on the board labeled "Alphabet Vowel Sounds" and "Relative Vowel Sounds." Direct students to form teams, and have them compete to find multi-syllable words for each column. After about five minutes, the team that comes up with the most words wins.

I Music of English
Class CD 1, Track 35

In addition to practicing stressed syllables and vowel sounds in context, this task provides practice with asking for directions, an indispensable skill in a foreign country.

> **Teaching tip** Since these are the longest Music of English lines encountered so far, you may want to use a new approach to introduce them. The technique of *backward build-up* can help students master the long sentences. In this technique, students begin with the last few words of the first line ("Where's the bank?") until they have grasped it perfectly. Then another chunk can be added to complete the line ("Excuse me. Where's the bank?"). This process can then be repeated with the second line, which you may want to break up into three or four chunks. For instance: "Selling Street"; "and Selling Street"; "Oater Road and Selling Street"; "the corner of Oater Road and Selling Street"; "It's on the corner of Oater Road and Selling Street." The advantage of this variation in approach is that students are moving forward into what is most familiar. However, since it is essential to keep the rhythm and linking right, you really have to concentrate on accuracy when modeling each chunk.

J Pair work: Asking about locations

This map game provides further practice with the One Vowel Rule and the Two Vowel Rule. Furthermore, it continues the theme of asking for directions by giving students an opportunity to adapt the little song they learned in Task I to various situations.

Remind students that, as they play the game, they may not use their hands to point to anything or to describe anything on the map. This is a considerable constraint for most students because it requires them to depend entirely on accuracy of pronunciation.

Although it is hard to estimate how much time to allow for this game, you will probably need to plan for at least 15 to 20 minutes. Students recognize the usefulness of the game and usually enjoy the total change of activity.

> **Teaching tip** A more playful approach to this task is to make a rough map on large rolls of paper taped to the floor (if this is possible in your classroom). Then students can direct each other to follow directions walking to a particular building.

K Dictation
Class CD 1, Track 36

Answer Key

1. Please remain seated.
2. Did you say "cheese" or "chess"?
3. We decided to attend the business meeting.
4. This is an expensive painting.
5. They closed all the shops on Wednesday.

Unit 3 Quiz is available on page 78.

Word Stress and Vowel Clarity

Unit overview

In this unit, students will learn how native English speakers use vowel clarity, in addition to vowel length, to add stress to a syllable. Within the context of this discussion, students will also be introduced to the English vowel sound *schwa*.

Clear vowels

It ought to come as good news to students that they do not have to pronounce every English sound clearly. In fact, they should not. This is because English speech depends upon the systematic distinction between clear sounds in the stressed syllables and less clear sounds in the reduced syllables. The vowel at the center of a reduced syllable is not only reduced in length, but it is also reduced in clarity. This reduced vowel is called "schwa," and it is an important key to the spoken language.

Schwa happens to be the most common vowel sound in the spoken language, but because it has no alphabet letter in the written language (other than the phonetic symbol /ə/ in dictionaries), it forms an immense barrier to listening comprehension for those students who have studied English through reading. At the same time, schwa is also a great barrier to literacy for those who have learned English through listening. It is not so important that students use schwa in speech, but it is *crucial* that they learn to recognize its presence when they're listening. When students practice saying schwa, it helps them hear it.

Vowels change in quality when they are reduced. The reduced vowel tends to be not only very short, but also very unclear, producing an obscure sound that is hard to identify. Consider, as an example, the name of the California town "Orinda," pronounced /ɔr•ˈɪn•də/, with the first vowel and the last vowel reduced to schwa. Only the second vowel in the word, the stressed vowel, maintains its clarity. The other two vowels are very unclear.

One American literacy tutor, on hearing about schwa for the first time, exclaimed, "You mean the vowel loses its integrity?" Vowel reduction is particularly baffling for students whose first language never reduces vowels, such as Spanish and Japanese. Toyama, a Japanese teacher

and colleague, had this to say about schwa: "Schwa is a modest vowel, who steps aside to let other vowels shine."

Note: In phonetics classes, students must distinguish among three reduced vowel sounds, but for practical ESL / EFL purposes, the term and symbol for schwa can be used for all of them.

A Clear vowels
Class CD 1, Track 37

This task presents the difference between a clear vowel and surrounding, unclear vowels.

B Schwa, the unclear vowel

Explain to your students that "reduce" means "to make something smaller or less important." This will help them understand the process of reduction as it applies to the English stress system.

C The contrast between schwa and clear vowels
Class CD 1, Track 38

Students should not repeat these words at this stage. Instead, direct them to listen and read along as you read the words or play the audio. The gray boxes help students visualize the contrast between the stressed vowel and the schwa-reduced vowel.

D Saying the contrast between schwa and clear vowels
Class CD 1, Track 39

Many languages are very careful to preserve the sound of each vowel in its clear form. That is why English vowel reduction is so foreign to most English learners. If English is spoken with all the vowels clear, it tends to confuse the native English-speaking listener because it obscures the stress pattern.

Answer Key

1. listen	6. arrange
2. reason	7. record (noun)
3. allow	8. American
4. attend	9. success
5. African	10. announce

E Pair work: Contrasting clear and reduced vowels

These words have been paired because they are particularly confusing for learners.

⌒ F Identifying and saying schwa
Class CD 1, Track 40

This task prepares students for Task G by showing them that some English words have syllables that are neither stressed (long and clear) nor reduced (schwa).

The following words from the list in the Student's Book all fall into this category:

photograph	/ˈfoʷ•tə•græf/
overcast	/ˈoʷ•vər•kæst/
economics	/ɛ•kəˈnɑ•mɪks/
application	/æ•pləˈkeʸ•ʃən/

Each of these words has a stressed syllable, a reduced syllable, and an ***unstressed syllable***, which is short yet nevertheless clear. Some books would refer to this type of syllable as having ***secondary stress***. For the sake of simplicity, however, *Clear Speech* presents the three levels of syllable stress as "stressed," "unstressed," and "reduced."

Answer Key

problém	photøgraph	ádoptéd
jackét	ovércast	applícatíon
extrá	ecónomics	cøllectéd
drámatic		

⌒ G Vowel length and vowel clarity
Class CD 1, Track 41

This task illuminates the three-way distinction revealed in Task F. Each of the three example words has one syllable that is stressed (long and clear), one syllable that is unstressed (short and clear), and one syllable that is reduced (short and unclear).

Call students' attention to the illustrations in the chart on page 28 of the Student's Book. The three figures in the chart represent the stressed, unstressed, and reduced vowels.

A much less ambitious, amusing approach, but one which requires a surprising amount of concentration, is to ask the group to say the words while being careful to raise their eyebrows as they say the stressed syllable. You could also add closed eyes for the reduced vowel.

H Identifying stress in multi-syllable words
Class CD 1, Track 42

This task is important as a preparation for Unit 5: Word Stress Patterns.

> *Answer Key*
>
> | | | |
> |---|---|---|
> | 1. attitude | 5. secondary | 9. constitution |
> | 2. institute | 6. reconsider | 10. understand |
> | 3. gratitude | 7. California | 11. distribution |
> | 4. military | 8. permission | 12. distributed |

I Limerick
Class CD 1, Track 43

If your students don't know what a limerick is, you might want to explain that it is a humorous poem with five lines, the first two lines having the same final sound as the last one.

Limericks and other light poetry are often helpful because they have highly controlled rhythm patterns, and they use rhyme to help students recognize those patterns. As with all the tasks in the Student's Book, you can determine whether or not the limericks suit your particular class.

> **Teaching tip**   One useful approach to limericks and poems is to assign them as homework. If students have memorized the words, they will be able to recite them without the struggle involved in reading out loud. This will encourage a more rhythmic and less monotone recitation.
>
> Begin with a choral recitation in class, so that no individual student will be put on the spot. You may, for instance, split the class in half and have the two halves recite alternating lines of the poem. You should take the role of the choral leader. By providing strong leadership and clapping a strong rhythmic pattern (or thumping a hand on the table), you can enable the class to stay together in a satisfying, confident way.
>
> Singing popular songs is a good extension of the limerick-type activities, but care must be taken to choose lyrics that both actually fit the rhythm of spoken English and are understandable without too much discussion of vocabulary.

J The vowel sounds in "can" and "can't"
Class CD 1, Track 44

This sound contrast is difficult to hear, even for native speakers of English. It is nevertheless motivating for students to work on hearing the contrast, because the difference in meaning is so obviously important.

L Music of English
Class CD 1, Track 45

Point out to students that the first two words in the question "What are you studying?" are contracted, so that they sound like "What're." The vowel sound in the word "are" is reduced almost to nothing. This is similar to the reduction that takes place in contractions like "I'm" and "she's."

M Check yourself: Stressed syllables
Class CD 1, Track 46

If you think the class may not be clear on how the topic of the lesson has been incorporated into this or any other dialogue task, you could read the dialogue out loud and point out the specific element being taught. However, the essence of the task is that it is an exchange between two people. This is crucial because language learners tend to focus their attention on avoiding mistakes, whereas they really should be thinking about the importance of helping the person to whom they are speaking notice the important points.

When students do dialogues in pairs, they should be required to change partners occasionally, as it is valuable for them to practice the skill of accommodating their ears to different voices and accents. Of course, if everybody in the class speaks the same first language, the accents will not vary much but the voices will be different, and this will help students learn to accommodate to variation.

> *Answer Key*
>
> A: What are you studying?
> B: Economics. What about you?
> A: Photography.
> B: Then you must take good photographs.
> A: And you must be good with money!

N Dictation
Class CD 1, Track 47

VOWEL WORK

This is the first Vowel Work section in the book. In addition to offering an opportunity for concentrated review of the sounds /iʸ/, /aʸ/, and /eʸ/, it also presents new decoding guidelines and introduces the concept of *linking*. Vowel Work sections like this one ensure that students will have opportunities to practice the alphabet vowel sounds and relative vowel sounds they have already learned. These sections also introduce additional vowel sounds and the most common spellings for them.

O The letters -y- and -w- as vowel sounds
Class CD 1, Track 48

The letters **-y-** and **-w-** share a special status within the English alphabet because they can act like either a vowel or a consonant letter. For example, the letter **-y-** sounds like a vowel letter in words like "creepy" and "rhyme," and it serves as a silent vowel letter in words like "ray" and "key." However, it is a consonant letter in a word like "you." The letter **-w-** also acts like a silent vowel letter in many words (e.g., "know," "low"), but it is a consonant letter in a word like "way."

> **Teaching tip** Encourage students to pronounce the words in the lists with long, clear vowels in the stressed syllables; with short, clear vowels in the unstressed syllables; and with short, unclear vowels (schwa) in the reduced syllables. This will help make a connection between this task and the material on word stress covered earlier in the unit.

P Linking vowels with an off-glide
Class CD 1, Track 49

Learners often have great difficulty identifying words when they are part of a natural stream of speech. When listening to spoken English, they often cannot tell when one word ends and another begins. This is because native English speakers do not normally speak with "spaces" between their words. The only people who do speak with "spaces" are language teachers trying to be helpful.

In spoken English, as in many other languages (e.g., French, Spanish), many words run together. That is, they link to each other without pauses between them. Because this is such a common and important characteristic of the language, ignorance of how linking works will severely limit learners' speech clarity and listening comprehension. The topic of linking will be presented various times throughout the remaining units of the Student's Book.

The linking pattern shown in this unit is that *front alphabet vowels* (the alphabet vowel sounds made toward the front of the mouth) are linked to other vowels with the off-glide /ʸ/.

Front alphabet vowel sounds: /iʸ/, /eʸ/, /aʸ/

> **Teaching tip** Write "Hi, everyone!" in large letters on the board. Then insert a superscript ʸ between the two words to show how this off-glide links the words together. Say the words and point out how, when said quickly, they sound like "Hiʸeveryone."

Q Using vowel symbols

This task combines practice with symbols, to focus attention on vowel clarity, while reminding students that the peak vowel is the peak of attention, and so must be clear.

Unit 4 Quiz is available on page 79.

5 | Word Stress Patterns

Unit overview

As mentioned in Unit 3 of this Teacher's Resource and Assessment Book, there is evidence to suggest that native English speakers store vocabulary items according to stress pattern (Brown, 1977, 1990; Levelt, 1989). This means that learning a word must include learning its stress pattern. It also means that when students say a word with its correct stress pattern, their listeners will find it easier to understand them, even if they do not pronounce each individual sound in the word correctly.

In this unit, students will practice a variety of English stress patterns. Inevitably, students learning about stress will ask their teacher for rules for assigning stress so that they will not have to learn words one at a time. Some systems for predicting word stress have been developed in the past, but they tend to be much too complex for practical use. This unit does not provide a long list of complex rules, but it does present a few practical principles and simple rules that will help students become more aware of their correct stress patterns.

If your students need higher-level work with word stress, use the tasks in Extra Practice 2, Part 1, on pages 164–166 of the Student's Book.

A Listening to stress patterns
Class CD 1, Track 50

This introduction is meant to reinforce students' understanding of the importance of stress patterns. It can be helpful to ask students to add some physical gesture, such as stretching a rubber band at the stressed syllables while saying the titles.

B Review: Identifying stressed syllables
Class CD 1, Track 51

This review task requires students to identify which syllable in a word is stressed, just as they did in Unit 4. Practice with listening for stress is a good way to instill in students the habit of noticing stress placement when learning a new word.

Answer Key

hamburger	extremely
cookies	accurate
pizza	dinner
refrigerate	electric
refrigerator	electrical
refrigeration	electrification

> **Teaching tip** One way to help students notice stress placement is to read a dialogue that the students can see in print, stressing the wrong syllable in some of the words. Ask the students to identify the words that you stressed incorrectly.

C Stress in two-syllable words
Class CD 1, Track 52

Words in print are separated by white spaces so that the reader can easily see where one word ends and another begins. In the spoken language, however, there are very few "white spaces" because words tend to run together. How then does the native English listener recognize the beginning of a word? Stress seems to provide a necessary clue, since a significant proportion of words (mostly nouns) are stressed on the first syllable.

> **Teaching tip** Ask students to help you make a list of well-known people (singers, actors, presidents, etc.) with two-syllable names, either first or last. Most two-syllable names will fit into the basic stress pattern presented in the Stress Rule for Two-Syllable Words, although some foreign-influenced names will not.

⌒D Stress in words that end in *-tion*, *-sion*, and *-cian*
Class CD 1, Track 53

1

Answer Key

reduction	electrician	participation
musician	complication	examination
correction	occupation	administration
permission	politician	contamination
instruction	regulation	organization

4

Answer Key

prediction	magician
vacation	election
education	commission
impression	aggravation

⌒E Stress in words that end in *-ic* and *-ical*
Class CD 1, Track 54

1

Answer Key

Atlantic	robotic	comic
majestic	narcotic	economic
domestic	statistic	dramatic
terrific	automatic	
Pacific	photographic	
diplomatic	democratic	

3

Answer Key

economical
technological
surgical
comical
political
chemical

⌒F Pronouncing two clear vowels together
Class CD 1, Track 55

Write some of the words from this list on the board, with dots separating the syllables (e.g., re•ality, ge•ography, ge•ology, cre•ate, recre•ation, associ•ation). This will help students see that, although the words contain vowels that are side by side, these vowels are, nevertheless, in different syllables.

⌒G Stress in two-syllable nouns and verbs
Class CD 1, Track 56

More than 90% of all English two-syllable nouns are stressed on the first syllable, and more than 60% of all English two-syllable verbs are stressed on the second syllable (Avery and Ehrlich, 1992). Since nouns vastly outnumber all other word classes, and since a high percentage of nouns have just one or two syllables, this tendency to stress the first syllable gives listeners a fairly reliable signal of the beginning of a word (Cutler and Norris, 1988).

This task helps students understand how stress can affect the meaning of a word by showing them that, in many cases, a change in stress can change a word's part of speech.

Here are a few more pairs:

Noun		Verb	
escort	/ˈɛs•koʷrt/	es**cort**	/ɪsˈkoʷrt/
protest	/ˈproʷ•tɛst/	pro**test**	/prəˈtɛst/
survey	/ˈsʌr•veʸ/	sur**vey**	/sərˈveʸ/

🎧 H Which word do you hear?
Class CD 1, Track 57

Audio Script

1. con**tract**	/kən'trækt/
2. **ex**port	/'ɛk•spoʷrt/
3. pro**gress**	/prə'grɛs/
4. **re**ject	/'riʸ•dʒɛkt/
5. **trans**port	/'trænz•poʷrt/
6. pre**sent**	/prə'zɛnt/
7. **con**flict	/'kɑn•flɪkt/
8. con**vert**	/kən'vərt/

Answer Key

Noun	Verb
1. con**tract**	(con**tract**)
2. (**ex**port)	**ex**port
3. pro**gress**	(pro**gress**)
4. (**re**ject)	re**ject**
5. (**trans**port)	trans**port**
6. pre**sent**	(pre**sent**)
7. (**con**flict)	con**flict**
8. con**vert**	(con**vert**)

🎧 I Stress in two-word verbs
Class CD 1, Track 58

Additional nouns and two-word verbs that you could write on the board are:

a **take**off (of an airplane)

take **off** (to fly off the ground)

a **send**off (a farewell party)

send **off** (to send someone or something somewhere)

a **print**out (paper copy)

print **out** (to make a paper copy)

🎧 J Music of English
Class CD 1, Track 59

Remind students that, for the word "suspect" in the first line, they should reduce the first vowel to schwa and make the second vowel long and clear. They should then reverse this stress pattern for the word "suspect" in the second line.

🎧 L Stress in compound nouns
Class CD 1, Track 60

Here are some other compound nouns that can be used for practice:

bedroom	passport
headphones	credit card
checkbook	book bag
headache	life jacket
teaspoon	night table

Additional, higher-level work on compound words is available in Extra Practice 2, Part 1, Task B, on page 165 of the Student's Book.

VOWEL WORK

🎧 N The spelling -ow- pronounced /aʷ/ as in "cow"
Class CD 1, Track 61

This Vowel Work task introduces a new vowel sound for the spelling -ow-. Because this is a new sound, it is a good idea to let students hear all the words in the list at least once before they are asked to begin listening and repeating. After students practice saying the words and sentences, you can direct them to think of more words that contain the /aʷ/ sound.

Here are some words that could be used:

vow	drown	flower
bow	clown	power
frown	shower	tower

🎧 O The spelling -ew- pronounced /uʷ/ as in "new"
Class CD 1, Track 62

Remind students that as they learned in Unit 2, the /uʷ/ sound is often pronounced /yuʷ/, as in "cube," and that "few" in the list is pronounced this way.

🎧 P Linking vowels with an off-glide
Class CD 1, Track 63

The concept of linking vowels, first presented in Unit 4, is continued here. In this unit, the linking pattern shown is that **back alphabet vowels** (the alphabet vowel sounds produced toward the back of the mouth) are linked to other vowels with the off-glide /ʷ/.

Back alphabet vowel sounds: /ɑʷ/, /oʷ/, /uʷ/

> **Teaching tip**   Write the words "Go under" on the board, using a linking mark to connect them. Say the words and point out that, when said quickly, they sound like "Go wonder."

🎧 Q Dictation
Class CD 1, Track 64

> *Answer Key*
>
> 1. He knows how to play the piano.
> 2. Every day there's a new conflict in the office.
> 3. Did you hear the reaction of the crowd?
> 4. Will she be in town for a few days?
> 5. I knew the politician would object.

For more advanced practice with word stress, see Extra Practice 2, Part 1, on pages 164–166 of the Student's Book.

Unit 5 Quiz is available on page 80.

6 Sentence Focus: Emphasizing Content Words

Unit overview

Units 3 through 5 dealt with the effect of stress on the rhythm of words. Unit 6 addresses the rhythm of whole sentences. Students will be introduced to the concept of *sentence focus* – the marking, by means of emphasis, of the word or words in a sentence that are most important.

∩ A Contrast
Class CD 2, Track 2

Students who are eager to be understood tend to think that every word is important, so they emphasize every word. Ironically, then, there is no easily identifiable focus of importance in what they say, and this makes it more difficult for listeners to understand them.

Even more damaging to understandability is when emphasis is misplaced. When this happens, listeners are faced with the task of first recognizing that something is wrong, and then backtracking to figure out what the focus of meaning really is (Hahn, 2004).

The pictures presented in this task visually illustrate the importance of emphasis. Tell students that when every word in a statement is emphasized, none of the words is easy to notice. Like the butterfly in the picture on the left, important information tends to blend in with less vital information. When a word is emphasized, it stands out, like the butterfly in the picture on the right, and is easier to notice.

∩ B Focus words
Class CD 2, Track 3

This task introduces the concept of focus word in the context of the pronunciation pyramid. If you haven't introduced the complete pyramid to the students yet, you might want to use this moment to do so.

This task also presents two possible melody patterns to ask the same thing. A jump up in pitch is probably more common, but in either case, the change in pitch calls attention to the focus word, whether it is up or down.

Intonation is commonly thought of as showing attitude. This is true, but it takes up a lot of classroom time to establish a context for a particular attitude, and the carryover to real communication is relatively limited. For practical language use, the most crucial function of English intonation is to highlight a focus word. Calling attention to the most important word helps the listener follow the speaker's meaning — it provides a navigational guide for the listener.

People have a tendency to speak a new language in a monotone, perhaps because they are insecure about speaking the new language. Another common tendency is for language learners to drop both the loudness and the pitch of their voice when they are uncertain about grammar or a vocabulary item. But pitch changes are so crucial for meaning in English that it is important for students to become consciously aware of how they are used for English purposes. Bolinger describes several signals for English emphasis (e.g., duration, pitch, and loudness) and concludes, ". . . there are reasons for believing that pitch is the one most heavily relied on" (1986, 21).

This task presents the first of seven Focus Rules, all of which are contained in Units 6 through 9. All of these Focus Rules are listed, for the purposes of review and reference, in Unit 9, Task J, on page 74 of the Student's Book.

> **Teaching tip** You can use a kazoo to help your students focus on pitch patterns and focus words. Using a kazoo will make the pitch change vividly memorable. It will help eliminate all the distractions of grammar, vocabulary, and individual sounds of spoken English, so that students concentrate on the "music."
>
> A kazoo is a toy instrument into which you can hum a melody. The kazoo amplifies the voicing sound made by the vibration of the vocal cords. Inexpensive kazoos are often available at toy stores or party shops. Students enjoy learning to use them. They are amused when they first see these toys, but they soon come to realize that these are serious tools for learning. If the price is too high for general distribution, you will find the kazoo useful as a demonstration tool and later, as a visual symbol of what needs correction.
>
> *Note:* Do not blow into the kazoo, as this produces no vibration of the vocal cords to amplify. You may, instead, say the vowel sound /uʷ/ and continue the sound as you put the end of the kazoo in your mouth. This will produce the desired humming sound.

🎧 C Music of English
Class CD 2, Track 4

This task practices the way the topic of the conversation shifts, as the focus words change.

🎧 D Finding the focus word
Class CD 2, Track 5

Students have already studied the need to make the vowel in the stressed syllable of a word extra long and extra clear. They have also learned how to make the other syllables in a word shorter and less clear. This contrast between a stressed syllable and the other syllables surrounding it creates the stress pattern of a word.

Now, students need to realize that all the words in a sentence are not equally important. Therefore, the stress patterns of every word in a sentence should not be equally noticeable. The only stress pattern that must be heard clearly is that of the particular word chosen for emphasis (the focus word). The other, less important words provide a background for the focus word, and their stress patterns do not have to be noticeable.

The focus word is central to the meaning of a sentence. To make sure that the listener notices that word, the vowel in the stressed syllable is not only lengthened and made extra clear, but a pitch change is added to the vowel. The reason for adding length to the vowel is, in fact, to make sure that the listener notices the pitch change.

> **Teaching tip**   You can use a kazoo to help your students understand pitch change and focus words as you did for Task B.

Answer Key

1. We'll be arriving <u>tomorrow</u>.
2. You look <u>great</u>.
3. She lives in <u>Toronto</u> now.
4. Is the baby <u>walking</u> yet?
5. Where are we <u>going</u>?
6. I'm always <u>hungry</u>.

🎧 E Music of English
Class CD 2, Track 6

> **Teaching tip**   If students have difficulty changing their pitch on the appropriate syllable, use a kinesthetic approach to support the raising of pitch. For example, ask students to raise their heads, hands, or eyebrows when they say the stressed syllable of each focus word. Another technique would be to have students stand up a little at their seats when they say the stressed syllables. This upward gesture tends to encourage "upward" pitch. Try it yourself. Singing a rising note while making an upward gesture actually feels natural. Singing a rising note while making a downward gesture, on the other hand, is surprisingly difficult.

F Focus and content words

Students naturally want to know rules for choosing focus words. One of the simplest rules is that the focus word is almost always a ***content word***. The distinction between ***content words*** and ***structure words*** is a universal division in all languages, but few people are consciously aware of these categories. You can help students become aware of the difference by saying that content words are "picture words." It is possible to visualize "book," "green," and "run," but no picture is likely to come to mind for structure words like "is," "the," or "it."

> **Teaching tip**   You can help Japanese students recognize the difference between content words and structure words by mentioning the difference between the *kana* and the *kanji* characters in written Japanese. The kana (characters representing syllable sounds) are generally used to "spell" structure words. The kanji (characters representing whole ideas) are generally used to convey content words.

G Content word game

If students have not recently studied English grammar, they may need to review the lists of nouns, main verbs, adverbs, etc. in Task F, in order to successfully complete Task G.

🎧 H Emphasizing the focus word
Class CD 2, Track 7

Because different languages use different means to call attention to the most important word, students need lots of practice using the English system.

I Adding the focus word

Possible answers:

1. swim, sing, go
2. bike, skateboard, horse
3. walking, laughing, talking
4. keys, papers, towel
5. expensive, hot, salty
6. where, when, how, why
7. well, fast, carelessly

J Pair work: Dialogue
Class CD 2, Track 8

This is another way to reinforce the attention on focus words.

Teaching tip One good way to illustrate emphasis is to bring a highlighter pen to class. Many students use these pens to highlight important words when they are studying, and "highlight" is more or less synonymous with "emphasize."

VOWEL WORK

K Review: Linking vowels with off-glides

This task provides a change of pace and gives students a chance to practice the linking patterns they learned in Units 4 and 5.

L Dictation
Class CD 2, Track 9

This task tests students' ability to comprehend sentences that contain vowels linked together by off-glides. You can also use the task to practice the topic of emphasis by asking students to underline the focus word in each sentence after they have taken dictation. The focus word in each sentence below has been underlined.

Answer Key

1. We all want the best solution.
2. Why are you asking me?
3. Tell me everything you know.
4. There's no snow anywhere.
5. Please show us the photographs.

M Review

The peak vowel at the top of the pyramid indicates that, in this case, "Toronto" is the focus word in this out-of-context sentence. If your students ask, you might want to tell them that depending on the context, the focus word could be another word in this thought group.

Answer Key

stressed syllable   ron
focus word   Toronto

Unit 6 Quiz is available on page 81.

7 Sentence Focus: De-emphasizing Structure Words

Unit overview

As explained in Unit 6, native English speakers use emphasis to create contrasts between important words and the less important words that surround them. Emphasizing the most important words makes them easier to hear. But in addition to emphasizing the most important words, native English speakers also *de-emphasize* the less important words, thereby making the contrast stronger. As one teacher expressed it, this is the difference between highlighting and dimming for a rock concert: to make something stand out, it is helpful not only to place a spotlight on it, but to obscure the background elements as well.

It may seem counterintuitive to teach students to think about elements in a sentence that need to be made less noticeable, but the contrast between the focus of meaning and the rest of a sentence is so crucial to intelligibility in English that learners need serious practice with learning to de-emphasize. Virginia Allen writes:

> Students (and sometimes teachers) ask, "But don't all languages use stress for signaling contrast and emphasis?" . . . The point is, in most other languages there is far less reduction of stress on the surrounding words, with the result that those words compete with the stressed element. . . . (1971, 81)

This difference between English emphasis patterns and those of most other languages makes teaching de-emphasis in English especially important.

This unit concentrates on various forms of de-emphasis that are commonly used in spoken English. These forms of de-emphasis are broken up into two categories: *contractions* and *reductions*. Unfortunately, it is common for students to be uneasy using any form of contraction or reduction, for at least two reasons:

1. They suspect that contractions and reductions are marks of sloppy speech used by uneducated people.
2. They feel some information is being left out when contractions and reductions are used.

These feelings form a barrier to learning, whether conscious or not. It is counterproductive to meet this resistance with repeated corrections, no matter how well meant, since students are apt to resist pressure to move in a direction they fear. Instead, it is far better and less threatening to introduce the topic as "useful for listening comprehension" and reassure students that they do not need to use contractions and reductions when they speak. In fact, it is better if they speak slowly when they really need to be understood, and reductions often sound peculiar in slow speech. However, students must learn to *hear* contractions and reductions easily, since most native English speakers use them often. Practicing to use contractions and reductions will help students "train their ears."

By the time students have completed Units 6 through 9 of the Student's Book, they should have an understanding of why contractions and reductions are a systematic part of spoken English. This understanding will certainly encourage them to use contractions and reductions themselves, but (and perhaps more importantly) even if students continue to speak in full forms, they will nevertheless have greatly improved their listening comprehension.

Note: The topics of contraction and reduction are repeated throughout the remaining units of the Student's Book.

A Focus and structure words

Focus Rule 3 presents the main source of contrast with the focus word.

The English learner's main difficulty with focus is not in learning how to emphasize the focus word, but in learning how to de-emphasize other words. It will help students to know that since the words chosen for focus are almost always content words, the *structure words* (e.g., articles, prepositions, etc.) that surround the content words are typically weakened or obscured. Students have already practiced reducing certain vowels in words, but now they need to learn to do this in sentences. This review of the terms *pronouns*, *prepositions*, etc., is especially helpful for students who have not studied grammar recently.

Practicing the reduction of structure words will help both with listening comprehension and intelligibility, since these words carry significant grammatical meaning but are characteristically hard to hear. For example, you may have noticed that structure words are often missing from students' speech and writing. This may be because these words do not exist in the same way in their first language, but it also may be because these words are not very noticeable in English speech.

> **Teaching tip** The following activity is suggested especially for use with advanced-level students:
>
> Explain what a telegram was and how it was used before the advent of email. Tell students that senders had to pay for each word they used, so they tended to send mostly content words. Structure words were not so important, so to save money the sender left many of them out. For example, a telegram reading "SEND MONEY BOUGHT CAR" meant something like "Send me money. I bought a car."
>
> Direct students, in pairs or small groups, to write a telegram based on the long message below. Ask them which words they cut out and which words they deemed essential.
>
> > The book that you ordered has arrived in our bookstore. Our address is 921 Main Street. The store opens at 10:00 a.m. and closes at 9:00 p.m. from Monday to Saturday. We are closed on Sundays. Your book will be kept for you at the customer service counter.

∩ B Music of English
Class CD 2, Track 10

You can refer back to the earlier template sentence, *How do you spell "easy"?* in Unit 6, Task B, on page 45 of the Student's Book to help students notice again how the structure words "do" and "you" are reduced to one syllable. In this Music of English task for Unit 7, Students will also notice that "don't" and "you" are reduced. Mastery of these templates gives the students a reference aid in their own long-term memory.

∩ C De-emphasizing structure words: Contractions
Class CD 2, Track 11

Contractions are introduced here by means of a listening activity in order to allay student anxiety about the topic. Once students are introduced to the concept of contraction, they soon begin to realize that contractions are part of the reason they feel native speakers speak too fast. Contractions are often made up of an auxiliary verb and another structure word (e.g., "D'you"). A failure to identify auxiliaries and pronouns can be particularly damaging to listening comprehension. Although the concept of contraction is fairly easy to understand, it is not at all easy to acquire the habit of recognizing these words in spoken English. Listening practice is, therefore, very useful.

Note: Students need to be told that contractions are not used in formal written English. Contractions convey an informality (mimicking speech) that is not appropriate for formal or academic writing.

> **Teaching tip** One way to present contractions visually is to show students two pieces of paper. One has the word "she" and the other has the word "is" (or similar words). Now bring these pieces of paper together so that the papers overlap and the "i" in "is" is covered up. This approximates the way these two words are usually spoken.

D Group work: Saying contractions

You can make this a very rhythmic exercise by conducting the choral response, like this:

1. Use your right hand to lead Group A (perhaps the right side of the class as you face them) to say "she."
2. Use your left hand to lead Group B (the left side of the class) to say "is."
3. Use both hands to bring everybody together to say the whole contraction "she's."
4. Immediately, without any break in rhythm, move on to "can," "not," "can't."

E Pair work: Saying contractions in sentences

> **Teaching tip** Advanced students can be asked to write their own sentence pairs in which the verb stays the same while contracted auxiliaries ("ve," "d," and "ll") are all that indicate the tense. Give them the following list of verbs, all of which can be used for this purpose:
>
> | | |
> |---|---|
> | let | put |
> | cost | quit |
> | cut | shut |
> | hit | spread |
> | hurt | wet |

F Saying common expressions with contractions
Class CD 2, Track 12

This task allows students to practice contractions and also introduces some highly useful conversational expressions. For those students who are already familiar with the expressions, the task provides an opportunity to analyze the familiar phrases in terms of how structure words are de-emphasized in them.

G Linking in common expressions
Class CD 2, Track 13

This is the first task to practice linking with consonant sounds. This is an important task because it helps prepare students for the linking patterns introduced in Tasks H through M.

H De-emphasizing structure words: Reductions
Class CD 2, Track 14

This task shows students how the vowels in some structure words are reduced to schwa when the words are de-emphasized. It also shows them that linking sometimes takes place as part of reduction. As mentioned earlier, it is good for students to know that, while they do not have to use such reductions in their own speech, it is important that they learn to hear them in the speech of other people.

I De-emphasizing structure words: Reduced "and"
Class CD 2, Track 15

In order for students to hear how reduction affects the rhythm of these phrases, say the phrase "cream and sugar" without reduced "and," pronouncing each sound clearly and without linking. Then say the phrase with reduced "and." Point out that when "and" is reduced, it fades into the background, rendering the other words more noticeable.

K De-emphasizing structure words: Silent letter -h-
Class CD 2, Track 16

The concept of silent -h- comes as a surprise to many students, but it explains a lot. Pronouns beginning with -h- are common ("he," "her," "his," "him"), and the silencing of this letter, combined with linking, often causes listening comprehension gaps. For instance, English learners may not be able to understand the words "Is he busy?" when they are pronounced with linking and reduction and therefore sound like one word: /ɪ•ziʸbɪ•ziʸ/.

> **Teaching tip** The *folded sentences* technique is useful for presenting the concept of silent -h-. On a long piece of paper, write sentences using pronouns that begin with the letter -h- (e.g., "Tell him something." or "Read her book."). Make two pleats in the paper so that the space after the first word, and the -h- in the next word, are eliminated when the paper is folded along the pleats. Show your students the full sentence, without folding the paper. Then fold the paper along the pleats so that the first two words look like one word (e.g., "Tellim" or "Reader"). This is an easy way to demonstrate an important difference between printed English and spoken English.

L Pair work: Linking over the silent letter -h-

Answer Key

2. a. Is her work good?   Yes, she does well.
   b. Is his work good?   Yes, he does a great job.
3. a. Give him a call.   I don't know his number.
   b. Give me a call.   OK, what's your number?
4. a. Did you take her pen? ·   No, it's mine.
   b. Did you take your pen?   No, I forgot.
5. a. Is this his apartment?   No, he lives upstairs.
   b. Is this Sue's apartment?   No, she lives downstairs.
6. a. Is he busy?   No, he isn't.
   b. Is she busy?   Yes, she is.

M Pair work: Dialogue
Class CD 2, Track 17

Answer Key

The Missing Singer

Stage Manager: Where's our singer?
Assistant: I think he's practicing, sir.
Stage Manager: But we need him on stage now!
Assistant: Well, you know how nervous he gets.
Stage Manager: Did you tell him the concert's about to start?
Assistant: He's practicing just as fast as he can.

N Limerick
Class CD 2, Track 18

Limericks and other light poetry are used occasionally in the Student's Book to take advantage of the way the swing of the rhythm reinforces reductions and contractions. This rhythm will be broken, however, if students have to pause at each line to figure out which words to emphasize. For this reason, it is better to have them read the poem first to themselves and underline the emphasized words before oral practice.

> ### Answer Key
>
> The three examples of "her" have the silent -h-.

O Dictation
Class CD 2, Track 19

If you choose not to use the audio, be sure to read these sentences to your students using contractions and reductions (e.g., silent -h-, reduced "and," etc.). It is not important, however, that students write down the contracted forms as they listen. After all, if students are able to hear the contraction "I'll," for example, and identify it as the contracted form of "I will," then it does not matter if they write down the contracted form or the full form.

> ### Answer Key
>
> 1. Did he give her the book?
> 2. I'll drive him to work.
> 3. We shared a sandwich and chips.
> 4. Where'd he go with your car?
> 5. I can't believe you don't own an umbrella.

VOWEL WORK

P The spelling -igh- pronounced /aʸ/ as in "night"
Class CD 2, Track 20

Students should find it welcome news that this spelling is so reliable as an indicator of the vowel sound. You could ask students to think of more words to put on the board. Here are some examples:

flight   fright   fight   light

Q The spelling -oo- pronounced /uʷ/ as in "moon"
Class CD 2, Track 21

This spelling is fairly reliable as an indicator of the vowel sound. Here are some more examples:

cartoon   spoon   doom   room

Unit 7 Quiz is available on page 82.

8 Choosing the Focus Word

Unit overview

As discussed in Unit 6, learners who are uncomfortable speaking English tend to speak in a monotone. Others may tend to emphasize every word, in the hopes of being understood more easily. Either approach degrades the intelligibility of their speech. Therefore, directing students' attention to the choice of focus words can make a considerable difference in understandability.

This unit presents rules that guide the choice of focus words at the beginning of a conversation and once a conversation is already underway. Students are also introduced to the concept of *contrastive emphasis*. This is the method by which native English speakers highlight a new piece of information (the *new thought*) by emphasizing it and thereby contrasting it with an old piece of information (the *old thought*) presented earlier in a conversation.

A Focus at the beginning of a conversation
Class CD 2, Track 22

Focus Rule 4 describes the "neutral" pattern for sentence focus in English. That is, a normal sentence that has no special contrastive meaning will usually have the focus on the final content word. That is the expected position for emphasis in English, and any change from that neutral position will call extra-special attention to the word emphasized.

This neutral pattern is natural for the first remark in a conversation, because nothing has been said previously that the speaker might want to contrast. Of course, a person might emphasize the first remark of a conversation in a special way. For instance, a person could begin a conversation by saying, "But what did JACK think about it?" In a case like this, we can assume that there was probably a previous conversation in which someone else's opinion was discussed, and both the speaker and listener are aware that their present conversation is taking place within the context of that earlier one.

Typically, however, focus at the beginning of a conversation follows the pattern described in Focus Rule 4.

> **Teaching tip**   If you have a kazoo available for Step 2 of this task, playing it is more effective than simply humming.

B Finding the focus word

This is a preliminary step. Some students still may need practice hearing emphasis and noticing which syllable is affected by it. If so, model the sentences for your students either before or after they have underlined the focus words.

> ### Answer Key
>
> 1. There's no elec**tri**city.
> 2. We need a **pho**tograph.
> 3. This is my **sis**ter.
> 4. Can I **help** you?
> 5. He doesn't under**stand** it.
> 6. Where did you **go**?
> 7. Open the **win**dow for them.
> 8. Please re**cord** this for me.

C Focus after the beginning of a conversation
Class CD 2, Track 23

The contrast between old thought and new thought is sometimes referred to as the difference between *old information* and *new information*. Whatever you might want to call it, the principle is that something is already understood between the two people talking (the old thought), and the speaker wants to call special attention to some other piece of information (the new thought).

All languages have one or more ways to show the difference between an old thought and a new thought, but English relies on intonation for this purpose more than most other languages do. Students, therefore, are likely to miss the spoken signals of contrast used by native speakers of English. When they learn to notice these intonation signals and recognize the implications, they make a major step forward in listening comprehension. At the same time, they greatly increase their intelligibility.

No intonational rules can account for all the potential feelings or intentions of a specific speaker in a specific context, so it is important for the student to develop a sensitivity to the speaker's efforts to highlight a particular word. The listener can then make a good guess about the purpose of the highlighting.

⌒ D Pair work: Dialogues
Class CD 2, Track 24

Each of these dialogues provides the opportunity for students to use contrastive emphasis. The first of the five dialogues (Step 1) serves as a template for the rest.

> ### *Answer Key*
>
> **A Traveler**
>
> | | |
> |---|---|
> | Travel Agent: | Where do you want to <u>go</u>? |
> | Traveler: | <u>Brazil</u>. |
> | Travel Agent: | <u>Where</u> in Brazil? To the <u>north</u> or to the <u>south</u>? |
> | Traveler: | <u>Neither</u>. I've <u>seen</u> the north and south. I'm going <u>west</u>. |
>
> **Two People on the Street**
>
> | | |
> |---|---|
> | Person 1: | What are they <u>building</u>? |
> | Person 2: | They're building a <u>school</u>. |
> | Person 1: | What <u>kind</u> of school? <u>Elementary</u> or <u>high</u> school? |
> | Person 2: | <u>Neither</u>. I think it's a <u>trade</u> school. |
>
> **A Tourist**
>
> | | |
> |---|---|
> | Tourist: | What's the best part of <u>Canada</u>? |
> | Canadian: | That <u>depends</u>. Do you prefer the <u>city</u> or the <u>countryside</u>? |
> | Tourist: | Well, I like <u>scenery</u>. |
> | Canadian: | Then you should go to the <u>Canadian Rockies</u>. |
> | Tourist: | Do they have good <u>shopping</u> there? |
> | Canadian: | Maybe you'd better go to <u>Toronto</u>. |
>
> **Two Students**
>
> | | |
> |---|---|
> | Student 1: | What are you <u>doing</u>? |
> | Student 2: | I'm <u>studying</u>. |
> | Student 1: | Studying <u>what</u>? <u>Math</u> or <u>English</u>? |
> | Student 2: | <u>Neither</u>. I'm <u>sick</u> of math and English. I'm studying <u>nutrition</u>, because I'm always <u>hungry</u>. |

⌒ E Music of English
Class CD 2, Track 25

This Music of English box shows how contrastive emphasis is used to correct something that was said before. The task helps prepare students for Task F by familiarizing them with a melody for disagreement.

Remind students to use a long, clear vowel and a pitch change for the stressed syllable of each focus word.

⌒ F Pair work: Disagreeing and correcting
Class CD 2, Track 26

Because ways of disagreeing are so culturally determined, students usually need to learn how to do this politely in other languages. This practice should help them learn how to do this politely in English.

H Pair work: Disagreement

> ### *Answer Key*
>
> *Possible answers:*
> 2. No, they're <u>cities</u>.
> 3. No, it's the <u>fifth</u>.
> 4. No, it <u>is</u> important.
> 5. No, it's a <u>big</u> country.

I What was said before?

Native speakers of any language quickly pick up clues about the topic of a discussion by listening to the vocabulary and the emphasis being used by the speakers. This helps them get oriented in the conversation quickly, even if they did not hear everything that was said before. Guessing backward is a great help in listening comprehension because it requires language learners to listen closely for these important clues and, thereby, become attuned to their presence and importance.

For a higher-level guessing backward task, see Extra Practice 2, Part 2, Task D, on page 169 of the Student's Book.

> ### *Answer Key*
>
> *Possible answers:*
> 2. The wedding is on the fourth of April.
> 3. We need less rain.
> 4. I prefer to keep the window closed.
> 5. Red is the best color for a car.
> 6. I think it's on page eight.
> 7. It's the left one.
> 8. It usually costs $25.

🎧 J Pair work: A disagreement
Class CD 2, Track 27

> **Answer Key**
>
> **Two Students Argue**
>
> A: I bought some books at the <u>library</u>.
> B: They don't <u>sell</u> books at the library. They <u>lend</u> books there. They sell books at the <u>bookstore</u>. Didn't you <u>know</u> that?
> A: On <u>Tuesdays</u> they sell books at the library. <u>Surplus</u> books.
> B: <u>Surplus</u>?
> A: Books they don't <u>need</u>. <u>Extra</u> ones.
> B: I didn't <u>know</u> that.
> A: There's a <u>lot</u> you don't know.

🎧 K Music of English
Class CD 2, Track 28

The melody practiced in this Music of English box is used to check information when something is not heard clearly or not understood. The use of emphasis to check information is further practiced in Task L.

> **Teaching tip** Any kinesthetic enhancement of emphasis can help students make the physical change in their throats needed to contrast the crucial syllable with the less important syllables in a sentence. If you have a class that enjoys team competition, they can benefit from the use of an activity developed by William Acton called "Syllablettes" (Acton, 2001). This is a more extended version of the task suggested in this book for Unit 4, Task G, for enacting word stress.
>
> Each team is given a sentence of no more than six or seven syllables, and each member is assigned a syllable. The teams then plan how to act out their sentence while saying it. For instance, students typically choose to have the schwas shrink, the stressed vowels spread themselves out to take up extra space, and the linking sounds link arms. Teams are often quite original in their choreography.
>
> Give the teams time to practice saying the sentence while acting it, until they can present it smoothly. The effect of the presentation can be something like "the wave" often seen in stadium stands, so this is particularly appealing to young students. The value of the activity is that the concentration required helps students overcome the instinctive tendency to transfer first-language rhythm into English.

🎧 L Pair work: Using focus words to check information
Class CD 2, Track 29

It is important for students to learn how to check information when they are not sure they heard something clearly, especially in a situation where instructions or directions are being given. This task presents and practices two strategies that students can use to confirm that they have heard something correctly or to request further clarification. For a higher-level task on checking information, see Extra Practice 2, Part 2, Task C, on page 168 of the Student's Book.

> **Teaching tip** These two-line dialogues can be practiced with what William Acton calls "The Walkabout," an activity in which students walk in a circle around the room, marking emphasis with longer steps (Acton, 2001). Olle Kjellin, who bases his teaching on the neurological value of choral repetition, wrote regarding this type of activity:
>
> I routinely use it in class. It is particularly useful for getting the unstressed syllables short enough. Initially, I do the walking myself in front of the class. Then the students join in, continuously "chanting" the practice sentence. After a while, I step aside and let the students pass by. Then I can easily monitor each one in turn, as they chant-walk past me, without having to interrupt the choral part of the exercise. (Kjellin, personal communication, 1991)

VOWEL WORK
🎧 M The vowel sound /ɔ/ as in "saw"
Class CD 2, Track 30

This Vowel Work task introduces the sound /ɔ/ and its most common spellings. Though this vowel sound is not used by speakers of every regional variety of English, it is nevertheless an important vowel for students to practice listening to.

🎧 N Dictation
Class CD 2, Track 31

> **Answer Key**
>
> 1. The wedding is in April.
> 2. The class begins at one.
> 3. What can we take for the party?
> 4. How many students are going?
> 5. Is the party at seven or eight?

Unit 8 Quiz is available on page 83.

9 Emphasizing Structure Words

Unit overview

In Unit 6, students learned that focus words are usually content words. In Unit 7, they learned how to reduce structure words so that focus words become easier to notice. Having become familiar with this basic emphasis pattern for English, it is important for students to also know that, in some instances, structure words are the focus of meaning and are, therefore, emphasized. Such emphasis generally highlights a contrast with something said previously during the course of an ongoing conversation.

Of course, it is possible to imagine a context where a structure word could be emphasized in the very first remark of a conversation. For instance, a friend could start a conversation by saying something like, "And what did HE say about it?" This would mean that both people had previously discussed the person that "he" refers to. This unit, however, concentrates on instances where a structure word is likely to be emphasized during the course of an ongoing conversation.

⌒ A Emphasizing structure words
Class CD 2, Track 32

Students tend to be uncomfortable with contractions and reductions because they think that information is somehow lost when words are reduced. Some students may also think that using reductions means speaking improper English. It is because of these common misconceptions that earlier units encouraged students to practice contractions and reductions (in order to improve their listening comprehension), but at the same time assured them that they do not need to use contractions and reductions in their day-to-day speech.

However, when students realize that structure words said in full, without contraction or reduction, are actually being highlighted as especially important, they may become more comfortable with de-emphasizing structure words when appropriate.

You may have noticed that structure words are typically missing in students' speech and writing. This may be because the function served by these structure words does not exist in the students' first language, or it may be because spoken English typically reduces these words, and students, therefore, have a hard time hearing them. Noticing the contrast between saying these words in a reduced form and in a full form can help students incorporate structure words into their mental template.

This task highlights the contrast between emphasized and de-emphasized structure words. It also presents a rule (Focus Rule 7), which will not only help students know when to emphasize a structure word, but will also help them understand why another speaker has chosen to emphasize one.

⌒ B Music of English
Class CD 2, Track 33

This task reinforces the reduction of "and" and the linking of "steak and" in the normal English emphasis pattern. It also presents an alternate emphasis pattern in which "and" becomes the focus word. Point out to students that while the "and" in the first line is reduced to /ən/, the "and" in the second line is pronounced in its full form, /ænd/, with a long, clear vowel sound. Also point out the rise in pitch on the second "and."

This Music of English box prepares students for the tasks that follow.

⌒ C Pair work: Emphasizing "and" and "can"
Class CD 2, Track 34

Because "and" and "can" are usually reduced, stressing them is a strong signal to native English speakers.

⌒ D Pair work: Emphasizing auxiliary verbs
Class CD 2, Track 35

This practice should help students recognize the significance of reducing vs. stressing these small words.

E Dialogue: Emphasizing "and" and auxiliary verbs

The structure words "and" and auxiliary verbs are so common in spoken English that learning to recognize them is a high priority for listening comprehension. Call students' attention to the difference between the reduced pronunciation of "do" in lines 1 and 2 and the long, clear vowel sound of "do" in line 5. Also point out that line 6 contains the contraction "I've" in place of "I have," but in line 7 the auxiliary verb "have" is pronounced in its full form, with a long, clear vowel.

Teaching tip   A different way to use a dialogue like this is to treat it like a dictation task. Direct students to close their books, and then dictate the dialogue while they write down what they hear. Another way to use dialogues is to assign them as homework for students who have equipment to record themselves. They can record themselves reading the dialogues and then listen to the recordings in order to monitor their own progress. If your students are unable to record the dialogue with a partner, they can do it on their own while playing both parts.

F Pair work: Emphasizing prepositions and pronouns
Class CD 2, Track 36

As in tasks above, this practice should reinforce the difference between reducing and emphasizing these kinds of structure words.

H Emphasizing pronouns
Class CD 2, Track 37

A few of the vocabulary items in this poem are likely to be unfamiliar to students. Here are some short definitions:

behold (line 1): look at
grim (line 3): very serious and sad
thou (line 5): old word for "you"

VOWEL WORK

K Different vowel sounds for the letter -a-
Class CD 2, Track 38

This listening task requires students to distinguish between three possible sounds for the letter **-a-**. Before doing the task, you may want to review the Two Vowel Rule and the One Vowel Rule in Unit 2, pages 12 and 14, and the spelling rules for the sound /ɔ/ in Unit 8, pages 67–68, of the Student's Book.

Audio Script

1. pawed	/pɔd/
2. pan	/pæn/
3. pawned	/pɔnd/
4. take	/teʸk/
5. balk	/bɔk/
6. stack	/stæk/
7. cat	/kæt/

Answer Key

1. paid	pad	(pawed)
2. pain	(pan)	pawn
3. pained	panned	(pawned)
4. (take)	tack	talk
5. bake	back	(balk)
6. stake	(stack)	stalk
7. Kate	(cat)	caught

L The contrast between /ɔ/ and /ɑ/
Class CD 2, Track 39

Although this task only requires students to distinguish between two vowel sounds, it is more difficult than the previous task because the two vowel sounds are so similar. After students finish circling the words they hear, you may direct them to practice saying the circled words.

Audio Script

1. stock	/stɑk/
2. dawn	/dɔn/
3. caught	/kɔt/
4. pod	/pɑd/
5. pond	/pɑnd/

Answer Key

1. stalk	(stock)
2. (dawn)	Don
3. (caught)	cot
4. pawed	(pod)
5. pawned	(pond)

M Dictation
Class CD 2, Track 40

The focus words in each sentence below are underlined.

Answer Key

1. I'm afraid I <u>cannot</u> agree.
2. Was it <u>his</u> or <u>mine</u>?
3. I think I'd like <u>both</u> salad <u>and</u> soup.
4. <u>No</u>, the key is <u>on</u> the desk, not <u>in</u> the desk.
5. <u>No</u>, it is <u>not</u> my fault.

For more advanced practice with sentence focus, see Extra Practice 2, Part 2, on pages 166–170 of the Student's Book.

Unit 9 Quiz is available on page 84.

10 Continuants and Stops: /s/ and /t/

Unit overview

You may wonder why the section on consonants begins with the sounds /s/ and /t/. The reason is that very few students have trouble distinguishing these sounds, so they are a useful pair for demonstrating the important difference between a ***continuant*** and a ***stop sound***.

Serious students and teachers often want to work on individual sound problems until they are mastered before going on to work on anything else. This can lead to a kind of "perfection trap," as explained by Joan Morley:

> At best, perfectionistic performance goals turn out to be unrealistic; at worst, they can be devastating: They can defeat students who feel they cannot measure up, and they can frustrate teachers who feel they have failed in their job. (1991, 498)

For this reason, the best approach is to present material, give students a chance to absorb the concepts and practice them, and then move on. You can then reassure them that these sounds will gradually improve as they learn to check their own performance.

Note: More difficult sound contrasts are presented in later units of the Student's Book. Extra Practice 1 on pages 145–163 of the Student's Book contains a number of additional tasks designed to practice consonant contrasts that cause particular difficulty for students from specific language backgrounds.

🎧 A Introducing continuants and stops
Class CD 2, Track 41

One graphic way to demonstrate the difference between continuants and stops is to say the word "bus," walking around the classroom and continuing the /s/ sound as long as you still have air in your lungs. Now say the word "but," without releasing any air after the final sound. At the end of the word, as you say the sound /t/, hold the palm of your hand up facing the class, in the nearly universal symbol for "Stop!" You can continue the /s/, but you must stop at the /t/.

In an effort to clarify the distinction between /s/ and /t/, teachers tend to release the /t/ sound with a little puff of air. Since at this stage it is important for students to understand the concept of stopping the flow of air, releasing the stop should be avoided.

As students listen to the words "bus" and "but," you can also direct them to notice the way the words are

presented in the gray pronunciation boxes. The shrinking final letters in "bus" will help students visualize how a continuant sound continues. The arrow and stop sign symbols below the words will also serve as reminders of how the two sounds /s/ and /t/ differ from each other.

Stop sounds in English:	/b/, /p/, /d/, /g/, /k/
Continuant sounds:	All other sounds, including vowels
Combined sounds:	/dʒ/, /tʃ/

> **Teaching tip**   When presenting the mouth drawings, take the time to encourage students to try the tongue positions silently. This silent practice should not be rushed because it is valuable preparation for actually making the sound out loud. Some students are helped by the pictures, but many are confused when they first see them. You can help them get oriented to a side profile picture of the mouth by drawing it on the board while they watch. Mention each part of the face (e.g., eye, nose, lip, etc.) as the chalk or pen line moves so they understand clearly which direction the profile is facing.
>
> When you get to the upper lip, ask students to touch the tip of their tongue to their own upper lip. Have them then follow with the tip of their tongue as you draw up in front of the upper teeth, down, then up again into the tooth ridge, and back onto the roof of the mouth. Since this activity is silent and invisible, it is private, so you will have a high level of participation. It draws students' attention to the parts you are mentioning in the most immediate way possible. No matter how unrealistic the sketch is, the students are getting a direct kinesthetic relationship to the drawing. This tongue-tip experience prepares them for later directions, such as "Press the tip of your tongue to the tooth ridge behind the upper front teeth" or "Press the sides of your tongue to the upper tooth ridge on the sides of your mouth."
>
> Also, call students' attention to the "Looking to the front" and "Looking down" drawings. These pictures aim to show how changes in airflow through the mouth create stop and continuant sounds. For instance, the "Looking to the front" view shows the narrow v-shaped passage through which air escapes the mouth when pronouncing /s/. The air passage is completely closed off for /t/.

While it is generally agreed that the beginning sound of a word is crucial to recognizing the word, this book gives higher priority to the final sound in words. This is because certain final sounds are necessary for clear grammar signals (e.g., a final /s/ or /z/ can mean "plural"). Also, many languages do not have final consonants, so students need to practice hearing and producing different kinds of consonants in this position. Concentrating on the stop / continuant contrast raises awareness of the existence of final consonants. Also, once students have a physical sense of the difference between stops and continuants, this contrast can be used to clarify a number of difficult sounds.

B Saying /s/ and /t/

Give students enough time to actually think about the tongue position differences in their own mouth and to experiment internally. Rushing through the explanation will slow down their absorption of the necessary feel of these sounds.

Whispering is a good alternative method of production because it changes the dynamics of the practice. It also allows students to try out the sound in a tentative, private way, before committing themselves to a production that others can hear. When people feel that their efforts are private, they can come closer to the target sound because they are not so worried about making errors.

> **Teaching tip**   One technique that can enhance a sense of privacy is to have students hold up a sheet of paper in front of their faces while they try out a new sound.
>
> Here are some more word pairs that may be used as part of this task:
>
> | ace | /eʸs/ | ate | /eʸt/ |
> |-----|-------|-----|-------|
> | yes | /yɛs/ | yet | /yɛt/ |
> | guess | /gɛs/ | guest | /gɛst/ |

⌢ C Which word is different?

Class CD 2, Track 42

Audio Script

1. lice, lice, light
   /laʸs/, /laʸs/, /laʸt/
2. base, base, bait
   /beʸs/, /beʸs/, /beʸt/
3. bat, bat, bats
   /bæt/, /bæt/, /bæts/
4. face, face, fate
   /feʸs/, /feʸs/, /feʸt/
5. boss, bought, boss
   /bɔs/, /bɔt/, /bɔs/
6. toss, toss, taught
   /tɔs/, /tɔs/, /tɔt/
7. pat, pass, pat
   /pæt/, /pæs/, /pæt/
8. coats, coat, coat
   /koʷts/, /koʷt/, /koʷt/

Answer Key

	X	Y	Z
1.			✓
2.			✓
3.			✓
4.			✓
5.		✓	
6.			✓
7.		✓	
8.	✓		

🎧 D Which word do you hear?

Audio Script

1. pat   /pæt/
2. bus   /bʌs/
3. cat   /kæt/
4. might   /maʸt/
5. rate   /reʸt/
6. nice   /naʸs/
7. boats   /boʷts/
8. face   /feʸs/
9. tickets /'tɪk•əts/
10. right   /raʸt/

Answer Key

1. pass   (pat)
2. (bus)   but
3. cats   (cat)
4. mice   (might)
5. race   (rate)
6. (nice)   night
7. (boats)   boat
8. (face)   fate
9. (tickets) ticket
10. rice   (right)

🎧 E Music of English
Class CD 2, Track 44

This Music of English box practices a useful question type for language learners. It also calls attention to the importance of the final consonant sound in English.

F Pair work: Singular and plural words

This task focuses students' attention on the fact that the final sound in a word can have grammatical meaning. This is particularly important for those students who have a tendency to leave off final consonants. It is also important practice for students who have difficulty with listening comprehension. The small difference between hearing a stop or a continuant can make a major difference in understanding what was said.

The use of hand signals instead of verbal responses not only adds a new dynamic to pair work tasks, but it makes it possible for you to quickly check on how well individual students are catching on.

Use this and other pair work tasks only to the extent that they are needed. If your students are doing them easily, either shorten the number of items in each task or skip it entirely.

🎧 I Linking with /s/
Class CD 2, Track 45

Different linking patterns will be presented and practiced in each of the next several units of the Student's Book (Units 11 through 14).

> **Teaching tip**   A memorable illustration is often more effective than hours of instruction. One way to wake up the class and help them understand and remember linking is to use magnets. Magnets are a useful metaphor for the irresistible attraction between succeeding words. To produce the effect, you need a very strong magnet and two blocks of wood. Paint or press vinyl letters onto the blocks to form two words, like "AT" and "ALL," in large capital letters. Use a strong glue to fasten the magnet onto the end of the first block and a flat piece of iron onto the second block. Now you can snap the words together and present them to the class. Students will find it hard to read the word "ATALL" until you break the blocks apart. The difficulty of reading linked words mimics the difficulty of hearing them.
>
> A simpler technique is to write the words on two pieces of clear plastic (a report cover will do) and slide them together over a piece of white paper. Words like "IS IT," for example, will look like "ISIT" and will, therefore, be hard to read. If you pull the clear sheets of plastic apart, the resulting white space instantly makes the words easy to read accurately.

🎧 J Linking with /t/
Class CD 2, Track 46

In addition to helping students understand running spoken English, linking practice can help students learn to pronounce difficult sounds. For example, in many cases, an English sound may exist in a learner's first language, but the rules of that language may only allow the sound to be used at the beginning of a word and never at the end of a word. With linking practice, the student's attention can be fixed on this sound as it transfers from the end of one word to the beginning of the next, thereby helping the student hear and say the sound in a new position.

This linking pattern (linking with /t/) and several others are practiced throughout the remaining units and in Extra Practice 1, Part 8, on page 163 of the Student's Book.

VOWEL WORK

⌒ K Practicing vowels with /s/ and /t/
Class CD 2, Track 47

Audio Script

1. at   /æt/
2. bought   /bɔt/
3. caught   /kɔt/
4. rate   /reʸt/
5. might   /maʸt/
6. boss   /bɔs/
7. mace   /meʸs/
8. lice   /laʸs/
9. mouse   /mɑʷs/
10. peace   /piʸs/

Answer Key

Words ending in /t/

1. ate   (at)   ought
2. bait   bat   (bought)
3. Kate   cat   (caught)
4. (rate)   rat   right
5. mate   meet   (might)

Words ending in /s/

6. base   bass   (boss)
7. (mace)   mass   mice
8. lace   lease   (lice)
9. moose   (mouse)   moss
10. pace   pass   (peace)

⌒ L Dictation
Class CD 2, Track 48

Answer Key

1. The tickets are in his pocket.
2. When will the maps be ready?
3. Did you say "book" or "books"?
4. Let's clean the mats and brass pot.
5. How do you spell "boss"?

Unit 10 Quiz is available on page 85.

Unit 10 *Continuants and Stops: /s/ and /t/*   **39**

11 Continuants and Stops: /r/ and /d/, /l/ and /d/

Unit overview

This unit continues to focus students' attention on the distinction between continuants and stops. In order to review the basic features of these two sound types, you may want to direct students back to Unit 10, Task A, in the Student's Book, where the concepts are introduced and explained.

🎧 A Continuants and stops: /r/ and /d/
Class CD 2, Track 49

The sound /r/ is difficult for students from many language backgrounds. In some languages, the /r/ sound is not a continuant, but is said by tapping or flapping the tip of the tongue on the roof of the mouth. This makes it sound a bit like /d/. Because of this tendency, learners of English often have difficulty making a clear distinction between words like "car" and "card" or, more importantly, between words like "fear" and "feared." Because the /d/ sound is a grammatical marker of the past tense, confusing it with /r/ can cause problems with speaking and listening comprehension.

At this point, some of your students may want to practice the difference between /r/ and /l/ because that particular contrast has been a worry for them. However, it is probably better to introduce these difficult sounds in contexts that are new to the students, to avoid reawakening what may be a long-felt sense of discouragement. That is why these two sounds are approached from different perspectives in this unit. The contrast between /r/ and /l/ may, however, be worth addressing with your students later. For exercises that directly address this sound contrast, see Extra Practice 1, Part 1, on pages 145–148 of the Student's Book.

Note: An /r/ sound tends to alter the preceding vowel, requiring a shift of the tongue. Notice, for instance, the difference between the vowel in "near" (/nɪr/) and the vowel in "need" (/niʸd/).

B Saying /r/ and /d/

The /r/ sound can be practiced with a small piece of paper placed in the mouth in such a way that the roof of the mouth is mostly screened off. Try this yourself. If the tip of the tongue reaches up to touch the roof of the mouth, the paper is a reminder not to touch. Keeping the paper in place, now try saying /d/. The feel of the paper makes clear the way the tongue must press against the tooth ridge all the way around to make this stop sound. The /r/ sound can and must be made without touching the paper at all.

> **Teaching tip** The name "Carol" can be compared with "cattle" or "kettle" as an example of the /r/ and /d/ contrast. This is because the letter -t- in between vowels is often said more like a /d/ than a /t/ sound. For more work on this "reduced -t-" phenomenon, see Extra Practice 1, Part 7, Task B, on page 162 of the Student's Book.

🎧 C Which word do you hear?
Class CD 2, Track 50

Audio Script

1. near	/nɪr/		5. deal	/diʸl/
2. feed	/fiʸd/		6. dome	/doʷm/
3. paid	/peʸd/		7. rent	/rɛnt/
4. core	/coʷr/		8. rave	/reʸv/

Answer Key

1. (near)   need
2. fear   (feed)
3. pair   (paid)
4. (core)   code
5. real   (deal)
6. roam   (dome)
7. (rent)   dent
8. (rave)   Dave

🎧 D Music of English
Class CD 2, Track 51

This Music of English box provides a good opportunity to remind students about sentence focus. Remind them to use a long, clear vowel and a pitch change for the stressed syllable of each focus word.

F Linking with /r/
Class CD 2, Track 52

Encourage students, when practicing the linked words in this task, to continue the **/r/** sound at the end of a word until they begin the next word.

Answer Key

1. Did you hear us?
2. There isn't a better answer.
3. I plan to retire early.
4. They share everything.
5. We're all here in the car.
6. Her answer is more interesting.

G Linking with /d/
Class CD 2, Track 53

Answer Key

1. I told everybody.
2. She said everything.
3. They made us do all the work.
4. The parade always starts early.
5. I did only the first part.
6. She had always wanted us to sing.
7. We tried our best.
8. Her grade is perfect.

> **Teaching tip**   Some or all of the sentences in Step 2 of this task may be used as part of a dictation exercise to help alert students to how well they are hearing the linked words. Here are some additional sentences for dictation:
> 1. My dad is moving the bed and the sofa.
> 2. She signed all the checks and paid every bill.
> 3. Would Alice help me build another one?

H The sound combination /rd/
Class CD 2, Track 54

This is a very challenging cluster of consonants for most students. Learning to hear it, however, is essential for efficient listening comprehension, since the distinction can mean the difference between a present and a past tense verb.

Audio Script

1. cheer	/tʃiʸr/
2. her	/hər/
3. shared	/ʃɛrd/
4. prepared	/prə'pɛrd/
5. hire	/haʸr/
6. retired	/rə'taʸrd/
7. bored	/boʷrd/
8. cared	/kɛrd/

Answer Key

1. (cheer)   cheered
2. (her)   heard
3. share   (shared)
4. prepare   (prepared)
5. (hire)   hired
6. retire   (retired)
7. bore   (bored)
8. care   (cared)

I Pair work: Past or present?

This task highlights the grammatical importance of a final **/d/** sound by focusing students' attention on how its presence or absence can change the meaning of an entire sentence.

If all the students in your class share the same first language, you may find that pair work tasks, like this one, that focus on specific target sounds might not be as effective as they would be in a multilingual class. This is because the students may automatically give each other clues about the sound, such as frowning or making an extra effort to pronounce the difficult sound clearly. Even if they cannot see each other's faces, the extra tension in the voice could give such an extraneous clue. If you have a feeling that this is happening, it might be better to concentrate on listening tasks, such as dictation.

J Continuants and stops: /l/ and /d/
Class CD 2, Track 55

The sound **/l/** can be confused with **/d/** because the tip of the tongue is involved in making both sounds. Students need to understand that unlike **/d/**, however, **/l/** is a continuant. When saying **/l/**, only the tip of the tongue is raised, thereby allowing air to flow out of the mouth.

If students can grasp the distinction between /l/ and /d/, as well as the distinction between /r/ and /d/ presented earlier, they will have a better chance later of controlling the difference between the /r/ and /l/ sounds.

For more work on the contrast between /r/ and /l/, see Extra Practice 1, Part 1, on pages 145–148 of the Student's Book.

🎧 K Which word do you hear?
Class CD 2, Track 56

Audio Script

1.	bed	/bɛd/	6.	did	/dɪd/
2.	said	/sɛd/	7.	date	/deʸt/
3.	spell	/spɛl/	8.	lime	/laʸm/
4.	failed	/feʸld/	9.	doom	/duʷm/
5.	maid	/meʸd/	10.	lawn	/lɔn/

Answer Key

1.	bell	(bed)
2.	sell	(said)
3.	(spell)	spelled
4.	fail	(failed)
5.	mail	(maid)
6.	lid	(did)
7.	late	(date)
8.	(lime)	dime
9.	loom	(doom)
10.	(lawn)	dawn

🎧 N Linking with /l/
Class CD 2, Track 57

Answer Key

2. Please tell us the news.
3. Are you well enough to work?
4. We have to pull up all the flowers before it snows.
5. I'll always call Allen on his birthday.

> **Teaching tip** The sentences in Step 2 of this task may also be used for a dictation exercise. Here are some additional sentences for dictation:
> 1. Did they steal all our money?
> 2. The hotel office will open at four.
> 3. I love cool evenings.

🎧 O Contractions with final /l/ and /d/
Class CD 2, Track 58

Many commonly used contractions in English end in /l/ or /d/. Since the final /l/ or /d/ can have a serious effect on meaning, it is important that students develop the ability to distinguish between them when they appear in this environment.

Audio Script

1. They'll ask a good question.
2. He'd answer soon.
3. Do you think they'll like it?
4. I said I'd do the work.
5. Who'll they ask?
6. Where'd Ann find one?

Answer Key

Full form
1. (They will)
   They would
2. He will
   (He would)
3. (They will)
   They would
4. I will
   (I would)
5. (Who will)
   Who did
6. Where will
   (Where did)

> **Teaching tip** These sentences can be used as part of a dictation task to help students test their own perception of the differences between the various contractions.

🎧 P The sound combination /ld/
Class CD 2, Track 59

These past tense verbs end in a consonant cluster of /l/ and /d/ sounds.

filled	/fɪld/		told	/toʷld/
sold	/soʷld/		spelled	/spɛld/
failed	/feʸld/		smiled	/smaʸld/
called	/kɔld/		sailed	/seʸld/

🎧 Q Music of English
Class CD 2, Track 60

Since the second line in this Music of English box is
rather long, you may want to teach its melody using the
backward build-up technique presented in the Teaching
Tip, Unit 3, Task I, on page 15 of this Teacher's Resource
and Assessment Book.

VOWEL WORK

S Using the Vowel Rules with /r/, /d/, and /l/

Here students are challenged to think about two different
topics at the same time. The task provides further
practice with /r/, /d/, and /l/ while also reviewing the
Vowel Rules introduced in Unit 2, on pages 12 and 14 of
the Student's Book.

🎧 T Practicing vowels with /r/, /d/, and /l/
Class CD 2, Track 61

Audio Script

1. fire	/fɑʸr/	
2. pure	/pyuʷr/	
3. hire	/hɑʸr/	
4. core	/coʷr/	
5. sad	/sæd/	
6. feed	/fiʸd/	
7. rode	/roʷd/	
8. ride	/rɑʸd/	
9. feel	/fiʸl/	
10. pale	/peʸl/	
11. mill	/mɪl/	
12. rail	/reʸl/	

Unit 11 Quiz is available on page 86.

12 | Voicing

Unit overview

The following is a true story. At an engineering conference in Kansas City, Missouri, two Americans took a colleague from Zurich to dinner. The Swiss engineer had rented a car and driven around the area the day before. Their conversation at dinner included the following exchange:

American 1: So, what have you found most interesting about Kansas City?
Swiss: The most interesting? It is the mice.
American 1: *(thinking of the hotel where they were all staying)* Mice???!!!
Swiss: Yes, that is clear. Here are much mice.
American 2: You mean . . . rodents?!
Swiss: *(unfamiliar with the term "rodents," does not respond)*
American 1: You've seen them?
Swiss: Oh yes, I saw them myself, all around the city.
American 2: *(trying a different approach, holds hands a mouse-length apart and then a rat-length apart)* Would you say they were this big or this big?
Swiss: *(holding one hand high above his head)* No, this big.

The two Americans only then realized that their Swiss colleague meant "corn." The term "maize" (which rhymes with "days") is used in British English but is not commonly used in North America. When a word like "maize" is pronounced in a Swiss German way, the letters **-ai-** sound like /ɑʸ/, and the final consonant is *voiceless*. As a result, the word sounds like "mice." This conversation was only temporarily derailed because the goodwill among the colleagues encouraged them to make the effort to get the discussion back on track. Oftentimes, however, a mistake like this can lead to a complete breakdown in communication.

The main point of this unit (and this story) is for students to learn that two contrasting sounds can be made with the tongue in exactly the same position, but with a contrast in *voicing*. Although many languages use voicing contrasts, the concept needs to be taught because it does not always transfer easily to a new language. In fact, this lesson may take extra time because so many sound problems can be traced back to the voicing distinction.

In a study of sound errors made by English language learners (Leahy, 1980), it was found that the two most common types of errors for individual sounds are based on continuancy (e.g., "bus" vs. "but") and voicing (e.g., "buzz" vs. "bus"). Interestingly, voicing errors with stop sounds (e.g., /d/ vs. /t/ and /b/ vs. /p/) were most often found to occur in the final position of a word. This particular type of voicing problem is addressed in Unit 13. Voicing errors with continuant sounds, however, were found to commonly occur in every position within a word.

🎧 A Introducing voicing
Class CD 3, Track 2

When learning to hear the difference between voiced and voiceless sounds, students are often told to cover their ears while producing a voiced sound such as /z/, and then contrast it with the corresponding voiceless sound /s/. This technique, however, is often not adequate. Instead, you should tell students to press their fingers firmly against their ears, closing the openings, in order to get the full effect of the contrast. Furthermore, the sound /z/ should not be pronounced "zee" (like the name of the letter -z-), but should be continued as "zzzz." That is why this task has students say the word "buzz" with a final extended /z/ sound. Similarly, the sound /s/ should first be said as the final part of a word, like "hiss."

Since the contrast between voiced and voiceless sounds is caused by the presence or absence of vocal cord vibration, another way to help students notice the difference is by asking them to lightly press a hand to the throat while alternating between /z/ and /s/. It is possible to feel the vibration or lack of vibration this way, but the distinction tends to be subtler than the sound difference created by tightly closing the ears. Try both of these demonstration methods yourself first to determine which one works best for you.

Teaching tip   Practicing while listening to and producing the contrast between voiced and voiceless sounds will help students learn the pronunciation of new or difficult words more easily. For example, present an unfamiliar word like "grisly" (pronounced with the voiced sound /z/). Ask students if the letter "s" is voiced or voiceless. Despite the spelling, the sound is voiced, and pronounced just like the word "grizzly." You may want to use a word that students are more likely to use in daily conversation, but this word was chosen because it is almost certain to be unknown. When students have learned to recognize the difference between voiced and voiceless sounds, this feature becomes an analytical tool for clearly hearing and mentally recording the pronunciation of a new word.

B Saying words with /s/ and /z/
Class CD 3, Track 3

The letters **-s-** and **-c-** do not always have their alphabet sounds. Students often ask if there is some kind of rule to determine whether the letter **-s-** should be pronounced as /s/ or as /z/ in a particular word. Unfortunately, the rules that have been developed are too complicated to be of practical use for English learners. However, the better students get at listening for the sounds, despite the spelling, the better they will also get at memorizing the pronunciation of common words that contain the letter **-s-** or **-c-**.

Teaching tip   This may be a good place to discuss the terms "Miss," "Ms.," and "Mrs.," which are all commonly used to address women. Considering the contrasts between these terms can make for an interesting analytical exercise.

Explain that:

- "Miss," pronounced /mɪs/, is a title for a woman who is unmarried. It is not common today except to formally address a young girl. The word ends in a voiceless sound.

- "Ms.," pronounced /mɪz/, is a title for a woman who is either married or unmarried. This word ends in a voiced sound.

- "Mrs." is pronounced with two syllables, as /ˈmɪ•səz/, and is a title for a married woman. It contains both a voiceless sound and a voiced sound. Furthermore, while "Mrs." is a short, three-letter abbreviation, it contains two syllables, while the other two terms only contain one.

By explaining the differences in meaning between these terms, you can reinforce in students' minds the importance of learning not only the distinction between voiced and voiceless sounds, but also the importance of using correct rhythm and syllable number.

Note: The pair "please / police" can also be used to analyze voicing contrasts, while at the same time reviewing syllable number and rhythm.

C Which word is different?
Class CD 3, Track 4

Audio Script

1. eyes, eyes, ice
   /aʸz/, /aʸz/, /aʸs/
2. buzz, bus, buzz
   /bʌz/, /bʌs/, /bʌz/
3. fuss, fuss, fuzz
   /fʌs/, /fʌs/, /fʌz/
4. phase, face, face
   /feʸz/, /feʸs/, /feʸs/
5. Sue, zoo, Sue
   /suʷ/, /zuʷ/, /suʷ/
6. seal, seal, zeal
   /siʸl/, /siʸl/, /ziʸl/
7. sink, zinc, zinc
   /sɪnk/, /zɪnk/, /zɪnk/
8. zip, sip, sip
   /zɪp/, /sɪp/, /sɪp/

Answer Key

	X	Y	Z
1.			✓
2.		✓	
3.			✓
4.	✓		
5.		✓	
6.			✓
7.	✓		
8.	✓		

⌂ E Saying phrases with /s/ and /z/
Class CD 3, Track 5

This task gives further practice distinguishing the sounds /s/ and /z/ and practices some of the phrases of the dialog in Task G.

⌂ F Music of English
Class CD 3, Track 6

This Music of English box contrasts the voiced and voiceless sounds /s/ (e.g., "that's") and /z/ (e.g., "amazing," "isn't") and also introduces a common pitch pattern for English tag questions (e.g., "isn't it?").

⌂ H The sounds /f/ and /v/
Class CD 3, Track 7

For students who have difficulty with the contrast between /v/ and /b/ or /f/ and /p/, it might be useful to review the continuant vs. stop difference (e.g., "rove / robe," "leaf / leap") before going into the voicing difference between /v/ and /f/.

For more work on the contrast between /v/ and /b/, see Extra Practice 1, Part 4, on pages 154–156 of the Student's Book. For work on the contrast between /f/ and /p/, see Extra Practice 1, Part 5, on pages 156–158 of the Student's Book.

⌂ I Saying words with /f/ and /v/
Class CD 3, Track 8

Before students listen and repeat, direct them to practice the position of the lips and teeth for /f/ and /v/. Practicing this mouth position is especially important for students who have difficulty distinguishing between the sounds /v/ and /w/. For work on this particular contrast, see Extra Practice 1, Part 3, on pages 152–153 of the Student's Book.

You can also help your students build confidence for this speaking task by encouraging them to whisper the words "leaf" and "leave" several times, until they become comfortable with the contrast.

⌂ L Voiced and voiceless sounds for the spelling -th-
Class CD 3, Track 9

Many languages do not have the sounds /θ/ (e.g., voiceless "thank") and /ð/ (e.g., voiced "this"), so learners tend to substitute another sound for each of these (e.g., /t/ and /d/, or, in some cases, /f/ and /v/). For more work on the contrast between /θ/ and the stop sound /t/, see Extra Practice 1, Part 6, on pages 159–161 of the Student's Book.

While /θ/ and /ð/ are technically called *interdentals* ("between the teeth"), they are not actually said with the tongue between the teeth. It is generally not a good idea to urge students to put the tip of their tongues between the front teeth to pronounce these sounds because in many cultures it is considered impolite, or even disgusting, to show one's tongue.

The most important aspect of the tongue position for both /θ/ and /ð/ is that it is relaxed and flat, so that air can flow out of the mouth without any hissing or buzzing noise. The tip of the tongue may briefly touch the back of the upper or lower teeth, depending on what kind of sound follows, but it rarely sticks out between the teeth.

Understanding the distinctive feature of *sibilance* (covered in Unit 14) will help clarify how these sounds are made, but in the meantime you may direct students to look at the mouth pictures for /θ/ and /ð/ in Extra Practice 1, Part 6, Task B, on page 159 of the Student's Book. Also, mirrors can be used to help students watch their tongue placement. Another advantage of a mirror is that it covers the mouth and thus gives the student some privacy. Self-consciousness is an enemy to pronunciation accuracy. If your students seem especially self-conscious, they may even benefit from practicing behind a sheet of paper held up in front of the face.

⌂ M Voiceless -th-
Class CD 3, Track 10

This task should help students hear this relatively quiet sound.

⌂ N Voiced -th-
Class CD 3, Track 11

If students have difficulty thinking about tongue position and voicing at the same time, direct them to stop up their ears as they did for Task A. This will help direct their attention to the presence or absence of voicing in the word list.

Audio Script

1. bathe   /be^{y}ð/
2. breath   /brεθ/
3. breathe   /bri^{y}ð/
4. math   /mæθ/
5. they   /ðe^y/
6. think   /θɪŋk/
7. thigh   /θɑ^y/
8. this   /ðɪs/

P Linking continuants
Class CD 3, Track 12

Encourage students not to pause between the linked continuant sounds.

For more work on this topic, see Extra Practice 1, Part 8, on page 163 of the Student's Book.

Q Review: Voiced and voiceless sounds for -th-
Class CD 3, Track 13

The distinction between the voiced and voiceless sounds is reinforced in this task.

R Pair work: Nouns and verbs

This task shows how the presence or absence of voicing in a final sound can sometimes change a word's part of speech. You may want to explain to your students that the noun "safe," used in the word list, sometimes means a strong box for valuables, like the ones used in banks.

The pyramids in this task show how sentences with a noun or a verb occasionally differ only in the final consonant of the word.

VOWEL WORK
T The vowel sound /ɔʸ/ as in "boy" and "coin"
Class CD 3, Track 14

Since the sound /ɔʸ/ only occurs in a stressed syllable, encourage students to make the sound long and extra clear for each word in the lists.

U Dictation
Class CD 3, Track 15

> **Teaching tip** If more voicing work is needed, have students dictate to each other from the lists of words in Tasks B, J, or R, choosing the voiced or voiceless version at random. This will enable them to give each other immediate feedback on the clarity of the distinction.

Unit 12 Quiz is available on page 87.

13

Voicing and Syllable Length
Aspiration

Unit overview

Students have already learned that it is important to lengthen vowels in certain syllables for stress and for sentence emphasis. Vowel lengthening, however, serves other crucial functions in English in addition to the ones already discussed. While many languages are spoken with roughly equal timing for all syllables, English rhythm is based on irregular syllable lengths, and one of the uses of lengthening in English is to let the listener know that a voiced consonant will follow. Even if a consonant is not heard clearly, the English listener can usually identify it correctly based on the relative length of the vowel that precedes it. Native English speakers acquire this skill at a very young age, in fact, because it is so important for listening comprehension.

It does not happen very often that a student immediately puts a lesson to good use, but the following story actually occurred. On a Monday, a workplace class in English pronunciation practiced vowel lengthening before a voiced consonant. On Tuesday, a Spanish-speaking member of the class called his local mechanic's garage to find out about the car he had left for repair. He asked over the phone, "Is Esteef there?" The mechanic said there was no such person at that number. The student thought back to the previous day's lesson and said, carefully lengthening the vowel, "Is Esteeeef there?" Although the Spanish pattern still produced an extra syllable and devoiced the final sound, the mechanic was now able to understand the request and said, "Oh, you mean Steve!" Business could then proceed. On Wednesday, the student reported this incident to the class, reinforcing Monday's lesson with a considerable tone of triumph. This was a happy day for the teacher.

Another topic in this unit is *aspiration*, which is introduced in Task N. In English, voiceless stop sounds (/p/, /t/, or /k/) at the beginning of a stressed syllable are distinguished by a little puff of air after the stop sound. This is a significant signal because in a high proportion of words the first syllable is stressed, so that aspiration is often a signal of the beginning of a word.

A Introducing voicing and syllable length
Class CD 3, Track 16

Explaining the importance of vowel lengthening before a voiced consonant will help motivate your students. Those who have difficulty with voiced sounds like /v/ and /z/

will be especially glad to learn about this extra clue offered by English to help listeners understand words even when the final sounds are not pronounced perfectly.

> **Teaching tip** Using a rubber band to show the contrast in vowel length will help some students grasp the concept more easily.

B Pair work: Final voiced and voiceless continuants

This is an important listening task because students usually do not realize that the length of a vowel is the main signal to distinguish the consonant that follows it. English learners from many first language backgrounds tend to devoice the final consonant in an English word, even when it should be voiced. If this happens, and the preceding vowel is not lengthened, then it becomes difficult for the English listener to understand the word correctly. The phonology rules of some languages tend to make all syllables short, causing a rather staccato rhythm. This pattern, when transferred to English, obscures the contrasts in syllable length that are so essential to clear English pronunciation.

C Which word is different?
Class CD 3, Track 17

> ### Audio Script
>
> 1. save, save, safe
>   /se^yv/, /se^yv/, /se^yf/
> 2. have, have, half
>   /hæv/, /hæv/, /hæf/
> 3. teeth, teeth, teethe
>   /ti^yθ/, /ti^yθ/, /ti^yð/
> 4. leaf, leave, leave
>   /li^yf/, /li^yv/, /li^yv/
> 5. raise, race, raise
>   /re^yz/, /re^ys/, /re^yz/
> 6. Miss, Ms., Ms.
>   /mɪs/, /mɪz/, /mɪz/
> 7. cap, cap, cab
>   /kæp/, /kæp/, /kæb/
> 8. back, bag, back
>   /bæk/, /bæg/, /bæk/

	X	Y	Z
1.			✓
2.			✓
3.			✓
4.	✓		
5.		✓	
6.	✓		
7.			✓
8.		✓	

D Final voiced and voiceless stops

It is common for teachers to release stop sounds at the end of words in order to make those final stops very clear. They might, for instance, pronounce a word like "stop" with a puff of air after the final /p/ so that students can hear the final sound more easily. Sometimes teachers even add a little vowel after the final sound (e.g., /stɑp•ə/). Since most native English speakers do not release these final stop sounds, it is better not to give this added clue to your students. Instead, students must learn to depend on the clues that actually occur in normal speech. Therefore, if you choose to model the words in this list for your students, use vowel length as a clue, instead of concentrating on the clarity of the final stops.

> **Teaching tip**   If you would like to review the topic of vowel length before voiced and voiceless stops, the words in this task can be used for dictation. Using a stretched rubber band as a visual reminder will help focus attention on the extra lengthening.

F Noun or verb?
Class CD 3, Track 18

This task reviews the common stress difference between nouns and verbs introduced in Unit 12, Task R, on page 106 of the Student's Book. This time, however, students should concentrate on vowel length, as opposed to hearing and producing the final consonants clearly.

1.	prove	/pruʷv/
2.	safe	/seʸf/
3.	teeth	/tiʸθ/
4.	excuse	/ɛk'skyuʷs/
5.	use	/yuʷz/
6.	believe	/bə'liʸv/
7.	devise	/də'vɑʸz/
8.	relieve	/rə'liʸv/
9.	grief	/griʸf/
10.	advice	/əd'vɑʸs/

1.	(prove) /v/	proof /f/
2.	save /v/	(safe) /f/
3.	teethe /ð/	(teeth) /θ/
4.	excuse /z/	(excuse) /s/
5.	(use) /z/	use /s/
6.	(believe) /v/	belief /f/
7.	(devise) /z/	device /s/
8.	(relieve) /v/	relief /f/
9.	grieve /v/	(grief) /f/
10.	advise /z/	(advice) /s/

H Pair work: Dialogue with voiced sound /z/ and voiceless sound /s/

Literal-minded students may argue that this is a nonsensical situation. Remind them that the point is to practice the lengthening distinction in sentences and that they should play it as comedy.

I Pair work: Giving directions

This task gives students the opportunity to review and practice language they will need to use for the map game in Task J.

Make sure students have enough time to practice the street names and the sample directions. Elicit the meaning of any unfamiliar vocabulary and add any other sample directions you consider necessary.

J Pair work: Map game

In addition to practicing the distinction between voiced and voiceless sounds, this task builds on the skills used for the previous map game (in Unit 3, Task J, on pages 22–24 of the Student's Book). While in the first map game students were required to ask about and describe the location of a building (i.e., "Excuse me. Where's the bank?" "It's on the corner of Oater Road and Selling Street."), here they face the challenge of asking for and giving detailed directions from one point to another. Remind the students that when playing the game they may not use their hands to point at anything or to describe direction. This is a considerable constraint for many people because it requires them to depend entirely on language.

It is hard to estimate how long the game will take, but you will probably need to allow at least 15 to 20 minutes of class time for it. It is generally a popular and productive exercise. Students recognize its usefulness, and they enjoy the total change of activity.

M Dictation
Class CD 3, Track 19

> ### Answer Key
>
> 1. What kind of seat is this?
> 2. She rode along the trail.
> 3. Who's ready to leave?
> 4. There's something in my ice!
> 5. There's something in my eyes!

N Aspiration: Contrasting voiced and voiceless stop sounds
Class CD 3, Track 20

Aspiration is a significant signal of stress, and may be easier for students to master than control for voicing at the beginning of a word.

Q Review: Aspiration

The pyramid shows how the aspiration comes with a stressed syllable, fitting in with the peak of meaning.

VOWEL WORK

R The spelling -ou- pronounced /ɑʷ/ as in "house"
Class CD 3, Track 21

Remind students that this is the same vowel sound they learned in Unit 5, Task N, on page 41 of the Student's Book.

Unit 13 Quiz is available on page 88.

14 | Sibilants

Unit overview

The term *sibilance* refers to the hissing sound that accompanies certain English consonants. This sound is the result of high-velocity turbulence in the air flowing out of the speaker's mouth. As the air flows through a narrow channel along the tongue, the friction caused creates a high-pitched "hiss." This hiss is a distinctive feature of the six English consonants known as *sibilants*: /s/, /z/, /ʃ/, /ʒ/, /tʃ/, and /dʒ/.

Many pronunciation difficulties can be aided by understanding the feature of sibilance. For example, English learners whose first languages do not have the sound /θ/ will often use the sound /s/ in its place. However, the sound /θ/ is not a sibilant, while /s/ is. Understanding sibilance and what causes it can help clarify the difference between these two sounds. Another example of the usefulness of understanding sibilance is the case of Japanese students, who sometimes add sibilance to a word like "he." As a result, English listeners will often mistake the "he," as said by a Japanese speaker, for "she." Understanding sibilance can also help speakers of Korean, who tend to add a vowel sound after final sibilants, and Spanish speakers, who tend to leave off the final /s/ or /z/ from plural nouns.

A Introducing sibilants
Class CD 3, Track 22

While students have practiced the sounds /s/ and /z/ in earlier units, this will be the first time they work on the other sibilants in a concentrated way. It is important, therefore, that they be allowed to listen to all the sibilants at this point in order to notice the hissing element in each one.

> **Teaching tip** One teacher has successfully used the following technique to demonstrate sibilance: Supply students with tiny coffee-stirrer straws. Direct them to hold the straw tightly with their lips, and then blow air through, being careful not to let any air escape from around the straw. This little exercise can help students understand the narrowness of airflow required to create sibilance.

B Saying sibilants

To distinguish between /s/ and /ʃ/, tell students to start from the /s/ position, with the tip of the tongue close to the front lower teeth and the sides of the tongue in

contact with the tooth ridge along the sides of the mouth. The narrow channel and the closeness to the front teeth cause the turbulence in airflow, which makes a hissing noise. Note that because this hissing sound is so high in pitch, it is especially difficult for people with hearing loss to notice it.

To change the /s/ to a /ʃ/ sound, draw the tongue back a short distance. The sides of the tongue should still be in contact with the side tooth ridge, but the tip of the tongue should no longer be close to the lower teeth. Round the lips to make a longer channel for the air to flow out. This longer channel makes a lower-pitched hissing sound.

Try these positions yourself before asking students to do it. Go back and forth between the sounds until you can clearly hear the difference in pitch.

Adding voicing to the above sounds to produce /z/ and /ʒ/ should be relatively easy at this point. However, if students are having a hard time adding voicing, practice should be discontinued before they get discouraged. The crucial point for them to master at this point is the presence of sibilance.

C Contrasting voiceless sibilants
/s/ (see) and /ʃ/ (she)
Class CD 3, Track 23

Here are some other pairs that can be used to contrast /s/ and /ʃ/ at the beginning of words:

sigh	shy
seal	she'll
suit	shoot
sign	shine
self	shelf

D Contrasting voiced sibilants
/z/ (zoo) and /ʒ/ (Asia)
Class CD 3, Track 24

Some students have a good deal of trouble distinguishing between these sibilants. Korean students, for instance, may use the same sound for /z/, /ʒ/, and /dʒ/. Practice with the tongue positions of the sounds will help students hear the sounds better.

∩ F Contrasting /s/ (sick) and /θ/ (thick)
Class CD 3, Track 25

Because /s/ is a common substitution for /θ/, this is helpful practice for making the distinction.

∩ G Contrasting /ʃ/ (ship) and /tʃ/ (chip)
Class CD 3, Track 26

Some students have difficulty hearing the difference between the initial sounds in "shoe" and "chew," and / or find it hard to distinguish the sounds in their own speech. This is often caused by the phonological rules of their first language, and it may take a good deal of practice for them to adapt to the English distinction.

It may be helpful to approach the distinction as a contrast between a stop and a continuant. Technically speaking, /tʃ/ and /dʒ/ are not stops, but combination sounds consisting of a quick stop followed by a continuant. The sound /tʃ/ is made up of a quick /t/ followed by /ʃ/, and the sound /dʒ/ is made up of a quick /d/ followed by /ʒ/. From a practical point of view, however, calling them stops will help students analyze the differences between these sounds and the continuants /ʃ/ and /tʃ/.

∩ H Contrasting /dʒ/ (jet) and /y/ (yet)
Class CD 3, Track 27

The contrast between the sounds /dʒ/ and /y/ can be explained in terms of two differences:

1. The sibilant /dʒ/ is a combination sound that begins with a short stop /d/ and finishes with the continuant /ʒ/.
2. The sound /y/ is not a sibilant. When making this sound, the air flowing out of the mouth is spread out across the top of the tongue, so there is no hissing.

> Teaching tip   Ask Spanish-speaking students to pronounce the spelling "ies" as if it were a Spanish word. This will help them produce a good English "yes."

J Linking with /tʃ/ and /dʒ/

Practice linking with the combination sounds /tʃ/ and /dʒ/ to a following vowel sound can help students notice the voicing of /dʒ/. This is because the final part of /dʒ/ is the voiced sound /ʒ/, which matches the voicing of the following vowel. In contrast, the final part of /tʃ/ is a voiceless /ʃ/ sound, which does not match the voicing of the following vowel. Therefore, there is a hissing noise in the link.

∩ K Music of English
Class CD 3, Track 28

This Music of English box contains several sibilants. Once students are done practicing the line, ask them how many syllables are in the plural words "oranges" and "slices." Then ask them how many syllables these words have in their singular form. Drawing attention to syllable number will help prepare students for Task L. You could substitute "wedges" or "ounces" for "slices," since the effect of the final sibilant adding a syllable is the same.

Note: Some native speakers of English say "orange" with one syllable; some say it with two syllables.

> Teaching tip   In order to prepare students for the lessons on *thought groups* in Unit 15, use a pause and change in pitch to separate the two thought groups when you model this sentence.

∩ L The -*es* ending and the number of syllables
Class CD 3, Track 29

The -**es** ending is as puzzling for students as the -**ed** ending can be, so this task helps reinforce the syllable number distinction depending on the preceding sound.

M Pair work: Sibilants and the number of syllables

At this point, it may be helpful to review the topic presented in Unit 1, Task F, on page 4 of the Student's Book, since that material was taught so early in the course. Remembering how the -**ed** ending adds an extra syllable to words that end in /t/ and /d/ can help students understand how the -**es** ending adds a syllable to words ending in sibilants.

> Teaching tip   An alternate way to conduct this task is to have Student A say a word from the lists, and then have Student B hold up one finger for one syllable or two fingers for two syllables. By taking turns, both students will have opportunities to practice speaking and listening.

∩ O Pair work: Dialogue
Class CD 3, Track 30

This task helps solidify students' command of the /s/ and /z/ distinction.

∩Q Tongue twisters with /s/, /ʃ/, /z/, and /θ/
Class CD 3, Track 31

Despite the challenge, students usually find this sort of task fun and useful.

∩S Dictation
Class CD 3, Track 32

Answer Key

1. Please don't put ice in my water.
2. She says that they're raising bees.
3. We'll all watch that TV program.
4. How many dishes of rice does she want?
5. Chips and jelly are a strange combination.

VOWEL WORK

∩T Difficult vowel contrasts
Class CD 3, Track 33

The vowel contrasts in this listening task cause difficulty for many students. Have students choose the contrasts that they find most difficult, and ask them to practice saying those words after they have listened to the audio.

Unit 14 Quiz is available on page 89.

15 Thought Groups

Unit overview

When we hear someone talking, we usually get the impression that the flow of speech is smooth and continuous. In reality, however, most speech is a sequence of brief stops and starts. These short sequences, or *thought groups*, are the result of efforts by the speaker to organize ideas by separating them into individual groups of words, so that the meaning of the entire utterance can be more easily understood. It helps the listener if the words related to each idea are grouped together.

Throughout the units, students have been repeatedly exposed to the idea of thought groups (mainly in the pyramids), presented as the foundation of the emphasis system. In this final unit, students are introduced to the way native English speakers use signals to mark the boundaries of individual thought groups. Before presenting these thought group signals, however, a brief review of focus emphasis is presented in Task A. Since the information in this unit is in many ways an extension of what was covered in Units 6 through 9, it is important that students be reminded of what they learned about focus words and how focus words are emphasized. You may want to refer students back to the review of Focus Rules in Unit 9, Task J, on page 74 of the Student's Book.

For higher-level students, you may choose to use some or all of the advanced thought group tasks found in Extra Practice 2, Part 3, on pages 170–173 of the Student's Book.

A Introducing thought groups
Class CD 3, Track 34

In English, thought-group boundaries are commonly marked by one or both of these basic signals:

- A pause at the end of a thought group
- A pitch drop at the end of a thought group

If you model the example sentence for your students, be sure to use a clearly marked pitch change and pause after each of these words: "apples," "grapefruit," and "peaches."

B Signaling the end of a thought group with a pause
Class CD 3, Track 35

Students need to be taught about thought group markers because languages differ both in the way thought groups are marked and in the concept of what should be included in a thought group. For instance, although many Indo-European languages use pauses to mark thought groups, many other languages (Cantonese, Korean, and others) use clause-final particles (affixes) and, therefore, do not need to rely on timing to indicate group boundaries. Furthermore, some languages that do use pauses to separate thought groups (French, Spanish, Japanese, Turkish, and others) normally put boundaries in places where native English speakers would not (Ballmer, 1980).

Because of these differences, students may not even notice pauses in the speech of others. But pauses are nearly as important as correct stress patterns and correct emphasis because they help guide listeners. For instance, if there are no pauses in the customary places, the native English listener may have difficulty understanding (mentally recording) a series of numbers, no matter how clearly each number is pronounced. In general, the "chunking" of language is a necessary mechanism to aid listener processing (Pribam, 1980).

C Using pauses with numbers
Class CD 3, Track 36

The pauses are a crucial part of making the number clear.

D Pair work: Using pauses in phone numbers

Other types of numbers may be used for this exercise, but the patterns of spacing may not be so simple. For instance, house addresses can be spoken in a number of ways. Social Security numbers and credit card numbers (or bank card numbers) have different spacing. Passport numbers usually are not spaced at all. It is useful to practice the spacing of telephone numbers since it is common for language learners and foreign travelers to have difficulty understanding or dictating phone numbers because they are not familiar with the grouping pattern. Different countries group their phone numbers differently.

E Pair work: Using pauses in math problems

If your students are used to dealing with algebraic equations, they will find it interesting and useful to practice reading them out loud. This can be done in the form of a student dictating equations to other students while they write what they hear on the board. The equations can begin with a simple "$(A \times B) + C = Y$" and become as complex as suits the ability of the class. If the thought groups are correctly indicated in the dictation, the equations on the board should be correctly written. This is another case where instant and highly practical feedback can aid learning.

F Signaling the end of a thought group with a falling pitch
Class CD 3, Track 37

Differences in intonational marking can cause a breakdown in communication. They can even cause bad feelings between people in instances where a listener misinterprets a speaker's intonation pattern. For example, some East Indian languages use a pitch fall as a signal that the speaker is about to make the most important point. Since the native English listener interprets the drop to mean "The end" or "Your turn to speak," there is apt to be serious misunderstanding. Unfortunately, people commonly mistake the intonation patterns of foreigners for insolence, indifference, or bad attitudes in general.

Falling pitch is an especially important signal for students to learn because, when speakers are talking quickly, they will often not pause at the end of a thought group. This means that the pitch change may be the only signal that a thought group has ended and another one has begun.

H Either / or questions
Class CD 3, Track 38

This task and Task I help students focus on the fact that both items linked by "or" are equally weighted and thus both are emphasized. Students should also notice that the questions have two thought groups.

J A series of items
Class CD 3, Track 39

This task helps reinforce the marking of each item in a list, so that the listener knows the list isn't finished until there is a drop in pitch.

K Saying a series of items

The Alphabet Game

As a class, take turns adding an item to the following sentence:

I'm going to New York and I'm taking . . .

The first item should begin with the letter **-a-**. The second item should begin with the letter **-b-**, and so on through the alphabet. Remember to make the pitch rise and fall on the last item. A student who cannot remember the whole list of items is out of the game. The next student should continue and add an item beginning with the next letter of the alphabet.

Example:

Student 1: I'm going to New York and I'm taking an apple.

Student 2: I'm going to New York and I'm taking an apple and a bicycle.

Student 3: I'm going to New York and I'm taking an apple, a bicycle, and a cap.

Student 4: I'm going to New York and I'm taking an apple, a bicycle, a cap, and a *(something that begins with the* **-d-***)*.

⌒ M Pair work: Dialogue using focus words in a series of thought groups
Class CD 3, Track 40

Teachers sometimes ask for rules to give their students about how to decide where to begin and end a thought group. Although linguists have been studying this question for decades, no one seems to have developed rules that are really practical for language learners. The best approach is to help students learn to hear the signals of thought grouping and think about grouping in their own speech. When students work in pairs or small groups to analyze a dialogue or a paragraph, their individual choices about grouping are likely to be different. Nevertheless, awareness is raised when they have to explain their choices.

Another task, similar to this one but more difficult, is included in Extra Practice 2, Part 3, Task D, on page 173 of the Student's Book.

Answer Key

Difficult Children

Mother:	We want a turkey and cheese <u>sandwich</u>, / and two <u>tuna</u> sandwiches. /
Server:	On <u>white</u>, / whole <u>wheat</u>, / or <u>rye</u>? /
Mother:	The turkey and cheese on <u>rye</u>, / and the other two on whole <u>wheat</u>. /
Daughter:	<u>No</u>! / <u>No</u>! / I want <u>white</u> bread! /
Mother:	Whole wheat's <u>good</u> for you. /
Son:	I want peanut butter and <u>jelly</u>, / not <u>tuna</u>! /
Mother:	<u>OK</u>. / One turkey and cheese on <u>rye</u>, / one tuna on <u>white</u>, / and one peanut butter and <u>jelly</u>. /
Server:	What would you like to <u>drink</u>? /
Mother:	One <u>iced tea</u> / and two glasses of <u>milk</u>. /
Daughter:	No <u>milk</u>! / <u>Lemonade</u>! /
Mother:	Three <u>sandwiches</u>, / one <u>iced tea</u>, / and two glasses of <u>water</u>. /

N Check yourself: Dialogue practice with thought groups

Answer Key

Possible answers:

Customer:	What can I have to <u>start</u> with? /
Server:	<u>Soup</u> / or <u>salad</u>. /
Customer:	What's <u>Super Salad</u>? /
Server:	What do you <u>mean</u>, / "Super Salad"? /
Customer:	Didn't you <u>say</u> / you have a <u>Super</u> Salad? /
Server:	<u>No</u>, / we don't have <u>anything</u> like that. / Just <u>plain</u> green salad. / Or you can <u>start</u> / with <u>tomato</u> soup. /
Customer:	Oh, / <u>OK</u>. / <u>Well</u> , / what do you have for <u>dessert</u>? /
Server:	We have <u>ice cream</u>, / <u>pie</u>, / and <u>apples</u>. /
Customer:	I don't <u>like</u> pineapples very much. /
Server:	Are you making <u>jokes</u> / or <u>what</u>? / We have <u>ice cream</u>, / <u>pie</u>, / and <u>apples</u>. /
Customer:	<u>OK</u>, / <u>OK</u>. / Just give me the <u>soup</u> / and a piece of apple <u>pie</u>. /
Server:	<u>Sorry</u>, / the only <u>pie</u> we have is <u>berry</u>. /
Customer:	Very <u>what</u>? /
Server:	<u>Excuse</u> me? /
Customer:	You said the pie was very <u>something</u>. / Very <u>good</u>? /
Server:	I said the pie was <u>berry</u> / – <u>blackberry</u>! / And if you will wait just a <u>minute</u>, / I'm going to get <u>another</u> server for you. /

> **Teaching tip** Advanced students can learn a good deal by recording a conversation of their own with somebody outside of a classroom setting, that is, in a live context. When listening to the recording later, they can transcribe some of the exchanges and then note where changing intonational emphasis and phrasing could have improved communication.

For advanced practice for both focus words and thought group marking, see Lectures for Listening Practice on pages 67–68 of this Teacher's Resource and Assessment Book.

O Analyzing a sentence

This final task with the pronunciation pyramid should help students review the main elements of spoken English they have practiced in *Clear Speech*.

> ### *Answer Key*
>
> 1.
>
> | | |
> |---|---|
> | peak vowel | /iʸ/ |
> | stressed syllable | speak |
> | focus word | speak |
> | thought group | Is it harder to speak |
>
> 2.
>
> | | |
> |---|---|
> | peak vowel | /ɪ/ |
> | stressed syllable | lis |
> | focus word | listen |
> | thought group | or to listen? |

P Review: Focus and thought groups

When students speak in class, they are typically thinking about avoiding mistakes in grammar, spelling, vocabulary, and so on. The one thing they are usually not thinking about is the listener. Native English listeners depend on pitch patterns and rhythmic signals ("road signs") to help them follow the intentions of the speaker, but English language learners typically do not use the signals that listeners are depending on. As a result, conversational breakdowns often occur. Emphasis that conveys the wrong meaning, or thought groups that either run together or break in inappropriate places, cause extra work for the listener, who is trying to follow the speaker's meaning. If the burden is too great, the listener simply stops listening. The great English novelist E. M. Forster expressed it this way: "A pause in the wrong place, an intonation misunderstood, and a whole conversation went awry." (from *A Passage to India*, 1924).

For this reason, students need to learn the importance of using rhythm and intonation to help the listener follow. This principle of "helping the listener follow" is so central to communication, in fact, that time spent helping students concentrate on the major rhythmic and intonational signals is more important than any other efforts to improve their pronunciation.

Unit 15 Quiz is available on page 90.

Appendix A
Parts of the Mouth

This illustration shows an interior side view of the mouth. Students are generally not consciously aware of what is happening inside their mouths, so looking at illustrations of different perspectives can help. The following procedure can help students orient themselves to the "geography" of the inside of their mouths. Before doing it, familiarize yourself with the drawing in Appendix A in the Student's Book on page 141 or in Unit 10 of the Student's Book on page 76. Give students time at each step to become consciously aware of the different parts of the *vocal tract*.

1 **Nose** – Draw just a nose on the board, facing to the right, the same way as in the illustration. Say "nose" as you draw it.

2 **Upper lip** – Continue the line down from the nose to draw an upper lip, saying, "upper lip." Ask students to touch the tip of their tongues to their upper lips. (There is no need for them to actually stick their tongues out beyond their upper lips.) Because this is a silent and private activity, even shy students should feel comfortable taking part. However, do not insist that students do this; they may simply wish to observe. After this, have students repeat after you the names of the parts so far: nose, upper lip, tongue, tip.

3 **Front teeth** – Continue the line, and draw the front teeth (rather v-shaped when looked at from the side). Say "front teeth," and ask students to follow with the tips of their tongues down the front of the teeth and up the back of the teeth.

4 **Tooth ridge** – Now extend the line slightly up and back from the teeth to show the tooth ridge (*alveolar ridge*). Say "tooth ridge," and ask them to follow this shape with their tongues, up over the bump behind the teeth and up to the roof of the mouth. Many English sounds are made by touching the tongue to the tooth ridge, for example, (/**n**/, /**l**/, /**t**/, or /**d**/). Other sounds are made by bringing the tongue near the tooth ridge, for example /**s**/ or /**z**/.

Appendix B
Tongue Shapes for /s/ or /z/, /t/ or /d/, /θ/ or /ð/, /r/, and /l/

Looking to the front

These drawings compare the mouth positions for some of the sounds practiced in the Student's Book. When students compare the sounds by looking at the differently shaped openings at the front of the mouth, they can see clearly that the airflow is different for each sound. The different configurations of the tongue shape the patterns of sound waves that the listener can hear as different speech sounds. Some of these configurations are easier to show from the side, and some are seen more clearly when viewed from the back of the mouth looking toward the front. That is why different views are shown throughout the Student's Book.

1 **/s/ or /z/** – These continuant sounds differ only in terms of voicing: /s/ is voiceless while /z/ is voiced. For both sounds, the tongue is v-shaped; air rushes through the narrow constriction formed by the tongue and hits the upper front teeth, making the hissing noise characteristic of sibilants. These two sounds are contrasted with each other in Unit 12 of the Student's Book. Unit 14 of the Student's Book deals with each of these sounds individually.

2 **/t/ or /d/** – The tongue position for these stop sounds is the same, but /t/ is voiceless while /d/ is voiced. For both sounds, the tongue blocks off air all the way around the tooth ridge (in a horseshoe shape). The sound /n/ is made the same way, but the air flows out through the nose. Unit 10 of the Student's Book contrasts /t/ with the continuant sound /s/. Extra Practice 1, Part 6, on pages 159–161 of the Student's Book contrasts /t/ with the continuant sound /θ/.

3 **/θ/ or /ð/** – These continuant sounds differ from each other only in terms of voicing: /θ/ is voiceless while /ð/ is voiced. For both sounds, the tongue is flat and air can flow out over it without any hissing. One way students can test this is to say each sound in a continuous stream of air and then reverse the airflow, drawing air back into the mouth. They should feel cold air flowing inward over their flat tongues. The sounds /θ/ and /ð/ are introduced and contrasted with

each other in Unit 12 of the Student's Book. Further work with /θ/ is provided in Unit 14 as well as in Extra Practice 1, Part 6, on pages 159–161 of the Student's Book.

4 **/r/** – For this continuant sound, the tongue is pulled back, and air flows over it without any stopping or hissing. This sound is covered in Unit 11 in the Student's Book and is contrasted with the sound /l/ in Extra Practice 1, Part 1, on pages 145–148 of the Student's Book.

5 **/l/** – For this continuant sound, the tip of the tongue touches the tooth ridge behind the front teeth, while the rest of the tongue is kept low, allowing air to flow out on either side. The sound /l/ is covered in depth in Unit 11 of the Student's Book. It is contrasted with the sound /r/ in Extra Practice 1, Part 1, on pages 145–148 of the Student's Book, and it is contrasted with the sound /n/ in Extra Practice 1, Part 2, on pages 148–151 of the Student's Book.

Looking down

The sounds /s/ and /t/ are common substitutes for the voiceless sound /θ/, and the sounds /z/ and /d/ are common substitutes for the voiced sound /ð/. This side-by-side comparison of the airflow and position of the tongue for these sounds should help students notice how they are produced differently.

It is important to give students enough time to absorb the information they can get from these illustrations. Encourage them to quietly try out the sounds over and over, or allow them to sit and think silently while they look at the pictures. Different students will benefit differently from the pictures.

Extra Practice 1
More Consonant Work

Overview

The tasks in Parts 1 through 6 of Extra Practice 1 work on consonant pairs that commonly cause difficulty for students from particular language backgrounds. Use these tasks as needed to address the specific needs of your students. Extra Practice 1, Parts 7 and 8, address two more topics related to English consonants: silent and reduced **-t-** and further work with linking.

Of course, it is not possible to address every potentially difficult consonant pair in Extra Practice 1. The six sound pairs included, however, represent some of the most common trouble areas. In order to address other problem pairs that you identify among your students, try to construct listening tasks with word pairs of your own. You may want to create new pairs using words from the existing activities.

Part 1   /r/ and /l/

🎧 A Listening to /r/ and /l/
Class CD 3, Track 41

In this task, students will hear the final and beginning sounds of /r/ and /l/ in several minimal pairs.

B Saying /r/ and /l/

If students have been reading English for some time and have difficulty saying /r/ or /l/, they may have developed a habitually wrong reaction to the letters **-r-** and **-l-**. Suggest to these students that they think of the letter **-r-** as short and bunched up, like the tongue is when drawn back for the /r/ sound. The /l/ sound is made with the tongue extended, reaching to touch the tooth ridge and shaped rather like the letter **-l-** itself but horizontal.

> **Teaching tip**   Here is a color-coded visual puzzle approach which may help overcome a "misreading" habit by giving students an unfamiliar presentation of the problem letters. Present students with a white poster on which you have written a number of words containing the letters **-r-** and **-l-**. Use black for all the letters except for **-r-** and **-l-**. For each **-r-** letter substitute a short, red square. For each **-l-** letter substitute a tall, yellow rectangle. Then ask different students to read the poster out loud. This puzzle presents the distinctive shapes of the letters but also adds a color term with the sound in it (e.g., "**r**ed" or "**yell**ow") to remind them which sound is which.

🎧 C Which word do you hear?
Class CD 3, Track 42

> #### Audio Script
>
> | | | | | | |
> |---|---|---|---|---|---|
> | 1. roll | /ro^wl/ | | 6. lock | /lɑk/ |
> | 2. hear | /hɪr/ | | 7. low | /lo^w/ |
> | 3. coal | /ko^wl/ | | 8. rate | /re^yt/ |
> | 4. steer | /stɪr/ | | 9. ram | /ræm/ |
> | 5. fail | /fe^yl/ | | 10. rhyme | /ra^ym/ |

> #### Answer Key
>
> | Final sound | | Beginning sound | |
> |---|---|---|---|
> | 1. (roll) | roar | 6. (lock) | rock |
> | 2. heal | (hear) | 7. (low) | row |
> | 3. (coal) | core | 8. late | (rate) |
> | 4. steel | (steer) | 9. lamb | (ram) |
> | 5. (fail) | fair | 10. lime | (rhyme) |

> **Teaching tip**   The following sentences can be used for dictation practice with the sounds /r/ and /l/.
>
> 1. It's hard to steer a car in the rain.
> 2. The core is in the middle of the apple.
> 3. The words "road" and "load" rhyme.
> 4. Did you see the fire?
> 5. A baby ram is a lamb.

Part 2   /n/ and /l/

🎧 A Listening to /n/ and /l/
Class CD 3, Track 43

In this task, students will hear the final and beginning sounds of /n/ and /l/ in several minimal pairs.

🎧 D Which word do you hear?
Class CD 3, Track 44

> #### Audio Script
>
> | | | | | | |
> |---|---|---|---|---|---|
> | 1. pine | /pa^yn/ | | 6. name | /ne^ym/ |
> | 2. coal | /ko^wl/ | | 7. nice | /na^ys/ |
> | 3. main | /me^yn/ | | 8. life | /la^yf/ |
> | 4. well | /wɛl/ | | 9. niece | /ni^ys/ |
> | 5. tune | /tu^wn/ | | 10. lot | /lɑt/ |

Answer Key

Final sound		Beginning sound	
1. (pine)	pile	6. (name)	lame
2. cone	(coal)	7. (nice)	lice
3. (main)	mail	8. knife	(life)
4. when	(well)	9. (niece)	lease
5. (tune)	tool	10. not	(lot)

> **Teaching tip** The following sentences can be used for dictation practice with the sounds /**n**/ and /**l**/.
>
> 1. The mailbox is on Main Street.
> 2. Did it rain last night?
> 3. We spent the night in a hotel.
> 4. When will you tell them?
> 5. We'll need a tool to dig the well.

F The sound combinations /nd/ and /ld/
Class CD 3, Track 45

In this task, students will hear the final sound combinations of /**n**/ + /**d**/ and /**l**/ + /**d**/ in several minimal pairs.

Part 3   /v/ and /w/

A Listening to /v/ and /w/
Class CD 3, Track 46

In this task, students will hear the beginning sounds of /**v**/ and /**w**/ in three minimal pairs.

C Which word do you hear?
Class CD 3, Track 47

Audio Script

1. while	/waʸl/	5. vain	/veʸn/
2. went	/wɛnt/	6. wishes	/ˈwɪ•ʃəz/
3. verse	/vərs/	7. we	/wiʸ/
4. veal	/viʸl/	8. vest	/vɛst/

Answer Key

1. vile	(while)	5. (vain)	wane
2. vent	(went)	6. vicious	(wishes)
3. (verse)	worse	7. -v-	(we)
4. (veal)	wheel	8. (vest)	west

> **Teaching tip** The following sentences can be used for dictation practice with the sounds /**v**/ and /**w**/.
>
> 1. I wonder if that's wise.
> 2. When will you visit again?
> 3. You can't grow vegetables without water.
> 4. We live west of the river.
> 5. They have always welcomed visitors.

Part 4   /v/ and /b/

A Listening to /v/ and /b/
Class CD 3, Track 48

In this task, students will hear the final and beginning sounds of /**v**/ and /**b**/ in some minimal pairs.

C Which word do you hear?
Class CD 3, Track 49

Audio Script

1. base	/beʸs/	6. robe	/roʷb/
2. bat	/bæt/	7. curve	/kərv/
3. berry	/ˈbɛ•riʸ/	8. carve	/kɑrv/
4. van	/væn/	9. dub	/dʌb/
5. vest	/vɛst/	10. jive	/dʒaʸv/

Answer Key

Beginning sound		Final sound	
1. vase	(base)	6. rove	(robe)
2. vat	(bat)	7. (curve)	curb
3. very	(berry)	8. (carve)	carb
4. (van)	ban	9. dove	(dub)
5. (vest)	best	10. (jive)	jibe

> **Teaching tip** The following sentences can be used for dictation practice with the sounds /**v**/ and /**b**/.
>
> 1. The cab is speeding around a curve.
> 2. I stood on the curb and waited for the bus.
> 3. You can't play baseball without a bat.
> 4. I don't believe you voted for Bob.
> 5. This vase looks very expensive.

Part 5 /f/ and /p/

⌒ A Listening to /f/ and /p/
Class CD 3, Track 50

In this task, students will hear the final, medial, and beginning sounds of /**f**/ and /**p**/ in three minimal pairs.

⌒ C Which word do you hear?
Class CD 3, Track 51

Audio Script

1. pool	/puʷl/	7. laugh	/læf/
2. fast	/fæst/	8. wipe	/wɑʸp/
3. put	/pʊt/	9. clip	/klɪp/
4. foal	/foʷl/	10. leaf	/liʸf/
5. fat	/fæt/	11. beep	/biʸp/
6. pace	/peʸs/	12. chap	/tʃæp/

Answer Key

Beginning sound		Final sound	
1. fool	(pool)	7. (laugh)	lap
2. (fast)	past	8. wife	(wipe)
3. foot	(put)	9. cliff	(clip)
4. (foal)	pole	10. (leaf)	leap
5. (fat)	pat	11. beef	(beep)
6. face	(pace)	12. chaff	(chap)

> **Teaching tip**   The following sentences can be used for dictation practice with the sounds /**f**/ and /**p**/.
>
> 1. They don't sell coffee at the copy shop.
> 2. Only a fool would jump in a pool in winter.
> 3. I walked past the house fast.
> 4. She purchased a new pair of fancy shoes.
> 5. She put pictures of pretty faces in a folder.

Part 6 /θ/ and /t/

One fairly common problem is the tendency to confuse the voiceless /**θ**/ with voiceless /**t**/, for example, saying "thank" as /tæŋk/. These two sounds differ from each other only in terms of the placement of the tongue. They are the same in terms of voicing.

Voiced substitutions follow the same principle, substituting /**z**/ for /**ð**/, for example saying "other" as /ˈʌ·zər/. A related problem from a different language background is substituting voiceless /**f**/ for voiceless /**θ**/ and voiced /**v**/ for voiced /**ð**/, especially between vowels.

For example, some students might pronounce "other" as /ˈʌ·vər/.

Here are a few minimal pairs that could be used to contrast these sounds:

thin / fin	than / van	that / vat
Ruth / roof	leather / lever	lithe / live
thought / fought	slither / sliver	with / whiff

⌒ A Listening to /θ/ and /t/
Class CD 3, Track 52

In this task, students will hear the final and beginning sounds of /**θ**/ and /**t**/ in several minimal pairs.

⌒ C Which word is different?
Class CD 3, Track 53

Audio Script

1. bath, bath, bat
   /bæθ/, /bæθ/, /bæt/
2. boat, boat, both
   /boʷt/, /boʷt/, /boʷθ/
3. math, math, mat
   /mæθ/, /mæθ/, /mæt/
4. path, pat, path
   /pæθ/, /pæt/, /pæθ/
5. Ruth, Ruth, root
   /ruʷθ/, /ruʷθ/, /ruʷt/
6. tank, thank, tank
   /tæŋk/, /θæŋk/, /tæŋk/
7. taught, taught, thought
   /tɔt/, /tɔt/, /θɔt/
8. thick, thick, tick
   /θɪk/, /θɪk/, /tɪk/

Answer Key

	X	Y	Z
1.			✓
2.			✓
3.			✓
4.		✓	
5.			✓
6.		✓	
7.			✓
8.			✓

Part 7   Silent -*t*- and reduced -*t*-

A Silent -*t*-
Class CD 3, Track 54

It is possible for students to guess what to write by identifying the sentences with the "be" verb, so you should ask them to wait to write until they hear the complete sentence.

Audio Script

1. We wanna go on a trip.
2. I wanna buy a car.
3. They wanna buy a present.
4. I think they're gonna leave.
5. Are you gonna show us your work?
6. What are you gonna do now?
7. I wanna study now.
8. Why do you wanna work so hard?
9. Because I wanna succeed.
10. Is she gonna be rich now?

Answer Key

1. We *want to* go on a trip.
2. I *want to* buy a car.
3. They *want to* buy a present.
4. I think they're *going to* leave.
5. Are you *going to* show us your work?
6. What are you *going to* do now?
7. I *want to* study now.
8. Why do you *want to* work so hard?
9. Because I *want to* succeed.
10. Is she *going to* be rich now?

Part 8   Practice with linking

These tasks can be used to reinforce the linking work that is presented at various points throughout the Student's Book. You may want to have students practice saying the phrases and sentences, or you may choose to use the sentences for dictation.

Extra Practice 2
Advanced Tasks

Overview

The tasks in Extra Practice 2 provide higher-level practice with word stress, sentence focus, and thought groups. Depending on the level of your class, you may choose to use these activities to supplement or replace some of the tasks in Units 1 through 15 of the Student's Book.

Part 1 Word stress

A Pair work: Practice with syllable number and word stress

This task is useful as a review of syllable number and rhythm. You may choose to use it with your class while working through Unit 5: Word Stress Patterns. On the other hand, you may choose to use it later to remind students about how syllable number and rhythm can affect the meaning of a word and, by extension, the meaning of an entire statement.

B Descriptive phrases and compound words

The topic of stress in compound words is first addressed in Unit 5, Task L, on page 40 of the Student's Book. If your students do well with that earlier task, you may want to use this task as well.

In Unit 5, Task L, students learn how to stress compound words that consist of two nouns (e.g., **rain**coat, **book**store, **light**bulb). Here they learn about the stress pattern for compound words that consist of an adjective + a noun (e.g., **hot** dog, **dark**room, **White** House). Note that the stress patterns for both categories of compound word are the same (i.e., the first part of the compound is stressed).

However, when an adjective is used to describe a noun as part of a phrase, the stress pattern is different. In cases like this, the **second** word gets the stress. Compare, for instance, the compound word "**light**house keeper" and the phrase "light **house**keeper." The two differ greatly in terms of meaning, but from a pronunciation standpoint, they differ only in terms of their stress patterns. The novelist Edna Ferber highlighted the way changes in stress can change meaning when she wrote the following comment about her housemaid, who happened to be a lighthouse keeper's daughter: "Housekeeping in a lighthouse must be light housekeeping indeed, for the housemaid's ideas on the subject were airy to the point of non-existence" (1940, 332).

> **Teaching tip** After working through Task B, you may want to present the following stress rules to your students. They address the difference in stress between compound nouns and compound verbs:
>
> 1. Compound nouns generally have the stress on the first part (**drug**store, **lunch** box, **weather**man).
> 2. Compound verbs generally have the stress on the second part (under**cook**, over**look**, out**run**).
> 3. Some compound nouns of location have the stress on the second part (New **York**, Times **Square**).

C Pair work: Saying stressed syllables in sentences

This task provides further practice with word stress patterns. Once students have completed the tasks in Unit 5 of the Student's Book, they may be ready for this one.

Part 2 Sentence focus

A Pair work: Focus words and the meaning of emphasis

This task is useful for students who have a firm grasp of the material in Units 6 through 9 of the Student's Book because it further alerts them to how the choices they make about emphasis will affect the way they are understood.

B Pair work: Focus words in a dialogue

Students may choose different focus words, and this is fine. What is most important is that they clearly emphasize the focus words they choose. The following answer key suggests possible choices for focus words.

> *Answer Key*
>
> **New York Cab Ride**
> Driver: Where <u>to</u>?
> Passenger: Times <u>Square</u>, please.
> Driver: Where are you <u>visiting</u> from?
> Passenger: <u>Chicago</u>.
> Driver: Yeah, that's what I <u>thought</u>, from the <u>accent</u>.
> Passenger: <u>Really</u>? I have an <u>accent</u>? Funny, I never <u>thought</u> about it. Where are <u>you</u> from?
> Driver: <u>Atlanta</u>.

Passenger:	Really? You're from the <u>South</u>? You don't <u>sound</u> southern.
Driver:	No, of <u>course</u> not. I'm studying to be an <u>actor</u>, and you can't have any <u>accent</u> if you want to be an <u>actor</u>.
Passenger:	So you just got <u>rid</u> of your southern accent?
Driver:	That's <u>right</u>. I wiped it out <u>completely</u>.
Passenger:	That's really <u>interesting</u>. I guess <u>that's</u> why you <u>sound</u> like you're from New <u>York</u>.
Driver:	I <u>do</u>?

C Pair work: Checking information

In Unit 8, Task L, on pages 66–67 in the Student's Book, students are introduced to the concept of emphasizing question words to check information. This task provides more practice with this important skill.

D Pair work: What was the question?

Because a question might not have been heard clearly, this task practices using the emphasis of the response to guess what must have been said before.

E What will come next?

Being able to predict what will be said next, based on the emphasis heard, is a very useful way to be sure that the listener is following the conversation. If what is said next does not match the listener's expectation, then a quick correction in understanding is needed. This can help avoid a continuing misunderstanding.

Part 3 Thought groups

A Road signs

The terms presented in this task are extremely important because they help speakers guide their listeners. When these "road sign" terms are used with their correct pitch patterns, they serve to clearly connect and punctuate ideas in ways that help listeners follow what is being said. They serve as "navigation guides" for the listener.

B Pair work: Monologue

As students read through this passage, they may choose different focus words and different places to put a slash. This is fine. What is most important is that they make thoughtful choices, and when they read the passage out loud, that they clearly emphasize the focus words they chose and use pauses and pitch changes to clearly indicate where thought groups begin and end.

The following answer key suggests possible choices for marking:

D Pair work: Road signs and parenthetical remarks

These common terms are meant to help the listener to follow the speaker's meaning. The most basic meanings are "more of what I just said" or "the opposite of what I just said."

Preparing for a Job Interview

A job interview, as you probably know, can be a pretty stressful experience. However, there are several things you can do to help ensure that an interview will run smoothly.

First of all, prepare yourself by learning as much as you can about the job you are applying for. Look for information about the company or organization online, for example, or speak to others who work in the same field.

Secondly, make a list of your relevant skills and experiences. Write down those things you have learned in school, for instance, or in other jobs that will help you be successful in the position you hope to fill. Then, try to memorize the skills and experiences you listed, so that you can refer to them easily during the interview.

On the day of the interview, leave yourself more than enough time to get there. You should try to arrive early or, at the very least, get there on time. After all, you do not want to rush into the meeting or, even worse, arrive late.

Finally, try not to be nervous. This, of course, is the hardest step of all. However, if you have made an effort to prepare yourself adequately, then you have every reason to approach the interview with complete confidence.

Lectures for Listening Practice

Following are two lectures. Read the lectures out loud, and ask students to take notes as they listen. They should not try to write everything they hear, but they should concentrate on catching the focus words. After each lecture, ask students to reconstruct what was said from their notes, either in writing or orally. This could be a good small group task.

A Age and Language Learning*

Most people think that the older you get, the harder it is to learn a new language. That is, they believe that children learn more easily and efficiently than adults. Thus, at some point in life, maybe around age 12 or 13, people lose the ability to learn languages well. Is this idea a fact or a myth?

Is it true that children learn a foreign language more efficiently than adults? On the contrary, research studies suggest that the opposite may be true. One report on 2,000 Danish children studying Swedish concluded that the teenagers learned more in less time than the younger children. Another report on Americans learning Russian showed a direct improvement of ability over the age range tested; that is, the ability to learn increased as the age increased from childhood to adulthood.

There are several possible explanations for these findings. For one thing, adults know more about the world and therefore are able to understand meanings more easily than children. Moreover, adults can use logical thinking to help themselves see patterns in the language. Finally, adults have more self-discipline than children.

All in all, it seems that the common idea that children are better language learners than adults may not be fact but myth.

B Thought Group Markers**

Today I want to tell you about some useful research on the way English speakers help their listeners. You know that a lot of English sentences are very complicated. The listener can get confused if the thought groups aren't clearly divided. If the thought groups aren't clear, the ideas won't be clear.

Each language has special ways to mark thought groups. In English, the chief marker is intonation. A researcher named O'Malley thought of a clever way to study these markers. He knew that algebra problems have to be written with parentheses. The punctuation marks are used to group the terms. If the algebra problem is spoken out loud, a native speaker of English can hear the grouping. Let me give you an example. Write down this equation:

$$A + (B \times C) = Y$$

Now write down another one:

$$(A + B) \times C = Y$$

Did you write the two equations differently? You should have put the parentheses in different places because the equations are different.

Perhaps you can get the idea better if I use examples from arithmetic. Write down this problem:

$$2 + (3 \times 4) = 14$$

Now write:

$$(2 + 3) \times 4 = 20$$

Did you put the parentheses in different places? The terms are exactly the same, but the groupings are different. That is why the answers are different.

The same concept of grouping also applies to words. Here's an example:

> "John," said the boss, "is stupid."

That has a very different meaning from this sentence, although it has the same words:

> John said, "The boss is stupid."

---

* Adapted from E. Hatch, "Optimal age or optimal learners?" *Workpapers in Teaching English as a Second Language,* Vol. X (1977): 45–56, and from S. Krashen, M. Long, and R. Scarcella, "Age, rate, and eventual attainment in second language acquisition," *TESOL Quarterly,* Vol. 13 (1979): 573–582.

** Adapted from M. O'Malley, D. Kloker, and B. Dara-Abrams, "Recovering parentheses from spoken algebraic expressions," *IIEE Transactions on Audio and Electro-Acoustics,* AU-21 (1973): 217–220.

The meaning is different, just as in the algebra and arithmetic problems. So grouping is important. Of course, speaking isn't like writing. We don't use parentheses or other punctuation marks when we're speaking. In fact, punctuation was invented to try to show some of the things we do in speech to separate groups of words. Written language substitutes punctuation marks for the spoken signals of intonation. The English listener depends on these intonation signals in order to understand clearly.

In his research on the subject of thought-group markers, O'Malley tape-recorded native English speakers reading algebraic equations aloud. Then he asked some other English speakers to listen to the recordings and decide where the parentheses were placed. O'Malley found that both the speakers and the listeners were very consistent in grouping the terms. The listeners were able to identify the placement of the parentheses because the speakers used three main markers to show the end of a group.

The first marker was *silence*. That is, the speaker paused after the group to make clear that it was finished. Listen for the pauses when I read this equation:

$$A \ldots + (B \times C) \ldots = Y$$

Marker 1, a pause, is quite powerful in slow speech. But in more rapid speech, there isn't time for many pauses. So the speaker has to rely on other signals to mark the end of a group.

Marker 2 is a change in pitch. Usually, the voice pitch drops low at the end of a group. Generally, a high pitch means a new group, and a low pitch means the end of a group. Listen for the pitch change when I read this equation:

$$(A + B) \times C = Y$$

Marker 3 is a lengthening of the final syllable of the group. Listen to the equation once more, this time paying attention to the lengthening of the final syllable in each group:

$$(A + B) \times C = Y$$

Other researchers[*] have confirmed these findings for spoken English. In both algebraic formulas and spoken English, the thought groups are divided with the same three markers. With marker 1, which is especially used for slow speech, the speaker pauses at the end of each group. With marker 2, the voice falls at the end of a group. With marker 3, the final syllable in each group is lengthened. For special clarity, all three markers are used.

I've reviewed some of this research because it shows a very important way to help our listeners understand us easily. The research demonstrates ways to make thought groups clear. Clear thought groups are part of clear speech.

---

* D. Klatt, "Vowel lengthening is syntactically determined in connected discourse," *Journal of Phonetics*, Vol. 3 (1975): 139, and I. Lehiste, "Isochrony reconsidered," *Journal of Phonetics*, Vol. 5, (1977): 253–263.

Tests and Quizzes

In the following pages, you will find photocopiable tests and quizzes and their audio scripts and answer keys. The audio for theses items is on the Assessment CD of the Class and Assessment Audio CDs component.

Clear Listening Diagnostic Test

The purpose of this listening test is to diagnose your students' ability to understand spoken English. How your students hear English is closely related to their ability to speak clearly. Beginning the course with this diagnostic test makes it possible for both you and your students to determine what areas of listening need improvement. You may also want to give the test again later in the course so that the students will have an objective measure of their progress. Of course, you should not give the test again until the students have been thoroughly exposed to the concepts in the Student's Book and have been given adequate time to practice them.

Photocopy the test on pages 70–73 for your students. When giving the test, you can either play the audio or read the test out loud, using the audio script on pages 91–92. Play the audio or read all the items twice. If you have advanced-level students, you can read all the items in the test only once (except the dialogue in Part 5 and the sentences in Parts 6 and 7).

The answer key for this test is on pages 91–92. This test is worth a total of 100 points. When you score the test, be strict. The purpose is to alert your students to the need for improvement so that they will pay attention to the lessons that follow.

Clear Speaking Diagnostic Test

The purpose of this speaking test is to diagnose what parts of your students' spoken English might tend to interfere with intelligibility. Beginning the course with this diagnostic test makes it possible for both you and your students to determine what areas of speaking need improvement. You may also want to give the test again at the end of this course so that your students will have an objective measure of their progress.

Photocopy the test on page 74, and have the students record themselves speaking the dialogue in this test. Then listen to the students' recordings while looking at a copy of the dialogue. Circle each error that you hear in the dialogue. You can use this information to fill out a personal pronunciation profile form for each student. (See below.) If your students do not have access to recording equipment, they could speak the dialogue directly to you, individually.

Pronunciation Profile

The purpose of this form is to help you and your students assess their English pronunciation abilities at the beginning of the course and measure their progress at the end of the course. Photocopy the form on page 75, and fill out one form for each student.

Unit Quizzes

The purpose of these quizzes is to give you and your students an indication of their progress in listening perception. This is closely related to clarity of speaking. You may give each of the quizzes after you have finished teaching the corresponding unit, or you may combine more than one quiz if appropriate.

Photocopy the quizzes on pages 76–90 for your students. When giving a quiz, you can either play the audio or read the quiz out loud, using the audio script on pages 93–100. To adjust to the level of your students, read slower or quicker depending on their ability to process what they hear. If you think your students need more time to process what is on the audio, you can pause the audio after each item to give your students more time to answer. Each task on a quiz is on a separate audio track, so you can play them twice if you feel the repetition would benefit your students.

The answer keys for these quizzes are on pages 93–100. Each quiz is worth a total of 20 points. If you need or want to give your students a grade, you can add up the scores for each quiz. Otherwise, you can simply mark the errors so that the students can see them.

Clear Listening Diagnostic Test

Name _____

Date _____   [____ / 100 points]

◎ Part 1 – Vowels

Listen. You will hear either sentence *a* or sentence *b* two times. Circle the letter of the sentence you hear. The first one is done as an example.

1. a. Did you bring the bat?
    b. Did you bring the bait?

2. a. I prefer this test.
    b. I prefer this taste.

3. a. It's a good bet.
    b. It's a good bit.

4. a. It's on the track.
    b. It's on the truck.

5. a. The men worked hard.
    b. The man worked hard.

6. a. How do you spell "scene"?
    b. How do you spell "sin"?

7. a. How do you spell "luck"?
    b. How do you spell "lock"?

8. a. We used a map.
    b. We used a mop.

9. a. Is John coming?
    b. Is Joan coming?

10. a. Everybody left.
    b. Everybody laughed.

11. a. I ran to school every day.
    b. I run to school every day.

[____ / 10 points]

◎ Part 2 – Consonants

Listen. You will hear either sentence *a* or sentence *b*. Circle the letter of the sentence you hear. The first one is done as an example.

1. a. Do you want everything?
   b. Do you wash everything?

2. a. They saved old bottles.
   b. They save old bottles.

3. a. She loves each child.
   b. She loved each child.

4. a. We'll put it away.
   b. We've put it away.

5. a. He spills everything.
   b. He spilled everything.

6. a. Does she bring her card every day?
   b. Does she bring her car every day?

7. a. What does "leave" mean?
   b. What does "leaf" mean?

8. a. Who'll ask you?
   b. Who'd ask you?

9. a. We wash all of them.
   b. We watch all of them.

10. a. He put the tickets away.
    b. He put the ticket away.

11. a. Is this the long road?
    b. Is this the wrong road?

[___ / 10 points]

◎ Part 3 – Number of syllables

Listen. Write the number of syllables you hear in each word.
The first one is done as an example.

1. easy   2
2. closet   ___
3. sport   ___
4. clothes   ___
5. simplify   ___
6. frightened ___

7. opened   ___
8. first   ___
9. caused   ___
10. Wednesday ___
11. arrangement ___

[___ / 10 points]

◎ Part 4 – Word stress

Listen. In each word, one syllable is stressed more than the others. Underline the stressed syllable you hear. The first one is done as an example.

1. requirement
2. political
3. photograph
4. photography
5. Canadian
6. geography
7. Europe
8. information
9. economy
10. economic
11. participating

[___ / 10 points]

◎ Part 5 – Emphasizing focus words

Listen. You will hear the following dialogue two times. In each sentence, one word is emphasized more than the others. Underline the emphasized word you hear. The first one is done as an example.

A: [1] Do you think food in this country is expensive?

B: [2] Not really.

A: [3] Well, I think it's expensive.

B: [4] That's because you eat in restaurants.

A: [5] Where do you eat?

B: [6] At home.

A: [7] You must like to cook.

B: [8] Actually, I never cook.

A: [9] So what do you eat?

B: [10] Usually, just cheese.

A: [11] That's awful!

[___ / 20 points]

Photocopiable

⊚ Part 6 – De-emphasizing with contractions and reductions

Listen. You will hear each sentence two times. Write the missing words you hear on the blank lines. The first one is done as an example.

1. Do you think _____ *she's* _____ OR _____ *she is* _____ in her room?
2. _____ you ask?
3. _____ work good?
4. Please _____ the information.
5. _____ want food?
6. How _____ you been here?
7. _____ Matt done lately?
8. Why _____ come so early?
9. _____ they gone?
10. We'd like some _____ vegetables.
11. They'll need _____ glasses.

[___ / 20 points]

⊚ Part 7 – Thought groups

Listen. You will hear either sentence *a* or sentence *b* two times. Circle the letter of the sentence you hear. Then answer the question that follows. The first one is done as an example.

1. a. John said, "My father is in the kitchen."
   (b.) "John," said my father, "is in the kitchen."
   Question: Who was speaking? _____ *my father* _____

2. a. The president shouted, "That reporter is lying!"
   b. "The president," shouted that reporter, "is lying!"
   Question: Who shouted? _____

3. a. She wants pineapples.
   b. She wants pie and apples.
   Question: What does she want? _____

4. a. Would you like a Super Salad?
   b. Would you like a soup or salad?
   Question: What were you offered? _____

5. a. We used wooden matches to start the fire.
   b. We used wood and matches to start the fire.
   Question: What was used to start the fire? _____

6. a. He sold his houseboat and car.
   b. He sold his house, boat, and car.
   Question: How many things did he sell? _____

[___ / 20 points]

Clear Speaking Diagnostic Test

Practice saying this dialogue until you are comfortable with it. Then record it or read it out loud to your teacher, speaking as naturally as possible.

Two University Students Meet

A: [1] Excuse me. Where's the library?

B: [2] It's on the corner of Main Street and Selling Road.

A: [3] Sorry, did you say Selling or Ceiling?

B: [4] Selling. It's directly ahead of you, about two blocks.

A: [5] Thanks. I need to buy some books for my classes.

B: [6] Oh, then you need the bookstore. You can't buy books at the library.
[7] You can only borrow them there.

A: [8] I guess I confused the words. They're different in my language.

B: [9] I know how it is. I get mixed up with Spanish words that sound like
[10] English words, but have different meanings.

A: [11] Are you studying Spanish?

B: [12] Yes, it's going to be my major. What are you studying?

A: [13] I'm studying English now, but my major will be economics.

B: [14] Really? My brother wanted to study economics. He took the
[15] entrance exam for that department just last week.

A: [16] Did he succeed?

B: [17] No, quite the opposite. He failed.

A: [18] That's too bad.

B: [19] Oh, it's OK. He would've had to study statistics, and he hated that idea.
[20] So now he plans to study music.

A: [21] That's great! Does he want to compose or perform?

B: [22] Both. He wants to compose and perform. He arranges programs for musicians,
[23] but he also plays classical guitar.

A: [24] Well, I wish him a lot of luck. And good luck to you, too. It was nice talking.

Pronunciation Profile

Name _____

Date _____

The checked areas need improvement.

1 Rhythm and word stress

___ Using the correct number of syllables

___ Stressing the correct syllable

___ Lengthening the vowel in a stressed syllable

___ Using a clear vowel in the stressed syllable

___ Using schwa in reduced syllables

___ Linking words

2 Emphasis and thought groups

___ Emphasizing focus words

___ De-emphasizing less important words

___ Grouping ideas into thought groups

3 Sounds

___ Using correct vowel sounds

___ Using correct consonant sounds

List of errors

_____

_____

_____

_____

_____

_____

_____

_____

_____

_____

_____

Unit 1 Quiz

A Listen. Write down the number of syllables you hear in each word.

1. entertain _____
2. support _____
3. invented _____
4. pleased _____
5. confused _____

[____ / 5 points]

B Listen. You will hear either sentence *a* or sentence *b*. Circle the letter of the sentence you hear.

1. a. They list all their tasks.
   b. They listed all their tasks.

2. a. Eric and Fred plant vegetables.
   b. Eric and Fred planted vegetables.

3. a. They need money.
   b. They needed money.

4. a. The fans applaud their team.
   b. The fans applauded their team.

5. a. Florence and Kay print their ads in the daily paper.
   b. Florence and Kay printed their ads in the daily paper.

[____ / 5 points]

C Listen. You will hear a sentence two times. Mark *Past* or *Present* for each sentence you hear.

	Past	Present
1.	_____	_____
2.	_____	_____
3.	_____	_____
4.	_____	_____
5.	_____	_____

[____ / 10 points]

Unit 2 Quiz

Name _____

Date _____   [___ / 20 points]

A Listen. Circle the word you hear.

1. goat   got
2. site   sit
3. feed   fed
4. rate   rat
5. cute   cut

[___ / 5 points]

B Listen. You will hear either sentence *a* or sentence *b*. Circle the letter of the sentence you hear.

1. a. If she's not careful, she's sure to fail.
   b. If she's not careful, she's sure to fall.

2. a. Of course we should aid her.
   b. Of course we should add her.

3. a. Which men do you mean?
   b. Which man do you mean?

4. a. Did you say "bite"?
   b. Did you say "bit"?

5. a. How do you spell "beast"?
   b. How do you spell "best"?

[___ / 5 points]

C Listen. You will hear a sentence two times. Circle the correct word you hear in the sentence. Then on the blank line, write the word from the box that has the same vowel sound as the word you circled.

/eʸ/ cake	/iʸ/ tea	/aʸ/ ice	/oʷ/ cone	/uʷ/ blue
/æ/ pan	/ɛ/ ten	/ɪ/ is	/ɑ/ top	/ʌ/ cut

1. I found the **pine** / **pin**.   _____
2. Where are the **beads** / **beds**?   _____
3. The man's **cape** / **cap** fell on the floor.   _____
4. Is that a new **coat** / **cot**?   _____
5. Tell us about your **plane** / **plan**.   _____

[___ / 10 points]

Unit 3 Quiz

Name _____

Date _____   [___ / 20 points]

◎ **A** Listen. Underline the stressed syllable you hear in each word.

1. sustain
2. confuse
3. problem
4. began
5. sensitive

[___ / 5 points]

◎ **B** Listen to the sentences. Underline the stressed syllable you hear in each word in bold.

1. That store is too **expensive**.
2. They live in **Washington**.
3. We believe there's too much **pollution**.
4. We're flying to **Brazil**.
5. That's a good **approach**.

[___ / 5 points]

◎ **C** Listen. You will hear each sentence two times. Underline the stressed syllable you hear in each word in bold. Then on the blank line, write the word from the box that has the same vowel sound as the peak vowel in that syllable.

/eʸ/	/iʸ/	/aʸ/	/oʷ/	/uʷ/
cake	tea	ice	cone	blue
/æ/	/ɛ/	/ɪ/	/ɑ/	/ʌ/
pan	ten	is	top	cut

1. The wedding will be **outside**.   _____
2. What is the best **method**?   _____
3. They signed an **agreement** today.   _____
4. Please don't **distract** me.   _____
5. We want to see a **parade**.   _____

[___ / 10 points]

Unit 4 Quiz

Name _____

Date _____

[___ / 20 points]

◎ **A** Listen. Draw a slash (/) through the vowel that is reduced to schwa. Each word has one schwa sound.

1. season
2. appeal
3. campus
4. promise
5. complain

[___ / 5 points]

◎ **B** Listen. You will hear either sentence *a* or sentence *b*. Circle the letter of the sentence you hear.

1. a. I can make it.
   b. I can't make it.
2. a. Jeff said he can do it.
   b. Jeff said he can't do it.
3. a. Can you give me a ride?
   b. Can't you give me a ride?
4. a. She can open the door.
   b. She can't open the door.
5. a. The driver can be there by three.
   b. The driver can't be there by three.

[___ / 5 points]

◎ **C** Listen. You will hear each sentence two times. Draw a slash (/) through the vowel that is reduced to schwa in each word in bold. Each word has one reduced vowel.

1. You need to **concentrate** harder.
2. This **photograph** is excellent.
3. What's her **telephone** number?
4. They live in **Washington**.
5. Those **women** work in the embassy.

[___ / 10 points]

Unit 5 Quiz

Name _____

Date _____   [____ / 20 points]

A Listen. Underline the stressed syllable you hear in each word.

1. reflection
2. inspection
3. statistic
4. practical
5. present

[____ / 5 points]

B Listen to the sentences. Underline the stressed syllable you hear in each word in bold.

1. We need an **electrician**.
2. That's a silly **generalization**.
3. He has strong **photographic** skills.
4. That student is studying **history**.
5. I **object** to that remark!

[____ / 5 points]

C Listen. You will hear each sentence two times. Underline the stressed syllable you hear in each word in bold. Did you hear a noun or a verb for the word in bold? Mark *Noun* or *Verb* next to the sentence.

	Noun	Verb
1. Did you say "**record**"?	____	____
2. How do you spell "**rebel**"?	____	____
3. What does "**import**" mean?	____	____
4. Did you say "**suspect**"?	____	____
5. How do you spell "**present**"?	____	____

[____ / 10 points]

Unit 6 Quiz

Name _____

Date _____   [___ / 20 points]

◎ **A** Listen. Underline the focus word you hear in each sentence.

1. You sing beautifully.
2. I can't find my keys.
3. We can't see it.
4. Are you angry with them?
5. I don't believe you.

[___ / 5 points]

◎ **B** Listen. You will hear the dialogue below two times. Underline the focus word you hear in each sentence.

Two Politicians Arguing

First Politician: [1] The public just doesn't agree with you.

Second Politician: [2] But my position is quite clear!

First Politician: [3] It doesn't seem clear to the public.

Second Politician: [4] Then maybe the public should listen better!

First Politician: [5] And maybe they don't want to!

[___ / 5 points]

◎ **C** Listen. You will hear each sentence two times. Underline the focus word you hear in each sentence. Then circle the stressed syllable in the focus word.

1. My cat refuses to eat fish.
2. I can't believe it!
3. He's a terrible driver.
4. This is a truly sudden decision.
5. That's an enormous expense!

[___ / 10 points]

Unit 7 Quiz

◎ **A** Listen. Draw a line through the reduced structure word you hear in each
sentence. Each sentence has one reduced structure word.

1. She wants eggs and toast.
2. Where will you put that?
3. She is sure to be famous someday.
4. Will he be here?
5. Has anyone seen him?

[____ / 5 points]

◎ **B** Listen. You will hear a sentence two times. Each sentence will have a
contracted form. Circle the letter of the full form of the contraction you hear.

1. a. We are
   b. We have

2. a. I have
   b. I will

3. a. We would
   b. We will

4. a. What have
   b. What will

5. a. They will
   b. They have

[____ / 5 points]

◎ **C** Listen. You will hear each sentence two times. Write the missing words you
hear on the blank lines.

1. _____ working hard.
2. _____ busy?
3. No, _____ not going.
4. _____ already gone.
5. _____ coming to the party?

[____ / 10 points]

Unit 8 Quiz

Date _____   [___ / 20 points]

◎ **A** Listen. You will hear either question *a* or question *b*. The underlined word in each question is the focus word. Circle the letter of the question you hear.

1. a. Is it a <u>big</u> dog?
   b. Is it a big <u>dog</u>?

2. a. Was it a tall <u>woman</u>?
   b. Was it a <u>tall</u> woman?

3. a. Who <u>wrote</u> that?
   b. Who wrote <u>that</u>?

4. a. Is the bear <u>hungry</u>?
   b. Is the <u>bear</u> hungry?

5. a. Where's my <u>cheese</u>?
   b. Where's <u>my</u> cheese?

[___ / 5 points]

◎ **B** Listen. You will hear the dialogue below two times. Underline the focus word you hear in each sentence.

Jan: [1] I love to exercise!

Jim: [2] I don't.

Jan: [3] But exercise is important!

Jim: [4] Yes, but I hate exercising.

Jan: [5] Then you should try playing a sport.

[___ / 5 points]

◎ **C** Listen. You will hear a question two times. Underline the focus word in each question. Then circle the letter of the answer that best fits the focus of each question.

1. Did the dog hurt his paw?
   a. No, he's just cleaning it.
   b. No, he hurt his jaw.

2. Was it an old man?
   a. No, it was a young man.
   b. No, it was an old woman.

3. Did you say that?
   a. No, my brother said it.
   b. No, I said something quite different.

4. Are you leaving at 10:00?
   a. No, at 9:00.
   b. No, I'm arriving at 10:00.

5. Is that John's report?
   a. No, it's Ellen's.
   b. No, it's his textbook.

[___ / 10 points]

Unit 9 Quiz

Name _____

Date _____   [____ / 20 points]

◎ **A** Listen to the dialogues below. Underline the focus word you hear in each B's response.

1. A: Did you put the key on the desk?
   B: No, I put it in the desk.

2. A: I don't think that's right.
   B: It is right.

3. A: Did you do that work?
   B: No, he did it.

4. A: We serve salad or soup.
   B: I want salad and soup.

5. A: You look tired.
   B: I am tired.

[____ / 5 points]

◎ **B** Listen. Each sentence will have a full form or a contraction. Circle the form you hear.

1. **We're / We are** taking the bus to work.
2. **I'm / I am** ready to leave.
3. **They've / They have** seen you at the mall.
4. **She's / She is** ready to go.
5. **We'll / We will** study your report.

[____ / 5 points]

◎ **C** Listen. You will hear the dialogue below two times. Underline the focus word you hear in each sentence.

A: [1] When is the next bus?
B: [2] Which bus?
A: [3] The bus to the mall.
B: [4] But there are two malls.
A: [5] I didn't know that. I want to go to the best one.
B: [6] Do you mean the best quality? Or do you mean the best prices?
A: [7] I want quality and low prices.
B: [8] Then you would have to take two buses.

[____ / 10 points]

Unit 10 Quiz

◎ **A** Listen. Circle the word you hear.

1. Kate   case
2. right   rice
3. note   nose
4. relate   relates
5. yet   yes

[___ / 5 points]

◎ **B** Listen. You will hear either sentence *a* or sentence *b*. Circle the letter of the sentence you hear.

1. a. Did you hang the cap up?
   b. Did you hang the caps up?

2. a. Turn the light off when you leave.
   b. Turn the lights off when you leave.

3. a. Please put your instrument away.
   b. Please put your instruments away.

4. a. Did you ask about the stock yesterday?
   b. Did you ask about the stocks yesterday?

5. a. Did she finish her plan on the economy?
   b. Did she finish her plans on the economy?

[___ / 5 points]

◎ **C** Listen. You will hear a sentence two times. Mark *Singular* or *Plural* for the last word you hear in each sentence.

	Singular	**Plural**
1.	_____	_____
2.	_____	_____
3.	_____	_____
4.	_____	_____
5.	_____	_____

[___ / 10 points]

Unit 11 Quiz

Name _____

Date _____   **[___ / 20 points]**

◎ A Listen. Circle the word you hear.

1. rave   Dave
2. liar   dire
3. expire   expired
4. fail   failed
5. let   debt

[___ / 5 points]

◎ B Listen. You will hear either sentence *a* or sentence *b*. Circle the letter of the sentence you hear.

1. a. Don't feed the animals.
   b. Don't fear the animals.
2. a. Did you dent this car?
   b. Did you rent this car?
3. a. We admired you.
   b. We admire you.
4. a. This bed is broken.
   b. This bell is broken.
5. a. We don't have any dimes.
   b. We don't have any limes.

[___ / 5 points]

◎ C Listen. You will hear a sentence two times. Write the missing words you hear on the blank lines.

1. _____ go tomorrow.
2. _____ they invite to the party?
3. _____ you stay on your vacation?
4. _____ study in the library.
5. I said _____ help you.

[___ / 10 points]

Unit 12 Quiz

Name _____

Date _____   [___ / 20 points]

A Listen. Circle the word you hear.

1. rise   rice
2. have   half
3. raising   racing
4. view   few
5. zip   sip

[___ / 5 points]

B Listen. You will hear either sentence *a* or sentence *b*. Circle the letter of the sentence you hear.

1. a. What blue eyes!
   b. What blue ice!

2. a. What are the prizes?
   b. What are the prices?

3. a. How do you spell "teethe"?
   b. How do you spell "teeth"?

4. a. How do you spell "ferry"?
   b. How do you spell "very"?

5. a. Whose van is it?
   b. Whose fan is it?

[___ / 5 points]

C Listen. You will hear the dialogue below two times. Circle the five words you hear that end in the /z/ sound.

Ann: [1] My brother likes fries.

Carol: [2] Does he like them with anything?

Ann: [3] Oh yes, with bananas.

Carol: [4] Is that the only odd combination?

Ann: [5] Well, he also likes peaches and ketchup.

[___ / 10 points]

Unit 13 Quiz

Name _____

Date _____   [___ / 20 points]

◎ **A** Listen. Circle the word you hear.

1. prove   proof
2. fuzz   fuss
3. lab   lap
4. sag   sack
5. kid   kit

[___ / 5 points]

◎ **B** Listen. You will hear either sentence *a* or sentence *b*. Circle the letter of the sentence you hear.

1. a. What's in the bag?
   b. What's in the back?

2. a. We rode on the bus.
   b. We wrote on the bus.

3. a. Did you say "have"?
   b. Did you say "half"?

4. a. Everyone loves peas.
   b. Everyone loves peace.

5. a. Please call me "Ms. Martin."
   b. Please call me "Miss Martin."

[___ / 5 points]

◎ **C** Listen. You will hear a sentence two times. Circle the correct word you hear in each sentence. Then on the blank line, write the consonant sound symbol for the last sound of the word you circled. Use these sound symbols: /s/, /z/, /d/, /t/, /b/, /p/, /g/, or /k/.

1. There's something in my **eyes / ice**!   _____

2. What does **"wrote" / "rode"** mean?   _____

3. Where's the yellow **cab / cap**?   _____

4. How do you spell **"debt" / "dead"**?   _____

5. Please define **"gap" / "gab."**   _____

[___ / 10 points]

Unit 14 Quiz

Name _____

Date _____

[___ / 20 points]

A Listen. Circle the word you hear.

1. mass   match   mash
2. pass   patch   path
3. chip   sip   ship
4. so   show   Joe
5. jet   yet   Chet

[___ / 5 points]

B Listen. You will hear either sentence *a* or sentence *b*. Circle the letter of the sentence you hear.

1. a. Did you watch the match?
   b. Did you watch the matches?
2. a. Write your name on the page.
   b. Write your name on the pages.
3. a. Put the books in the box.
   b. Put the books in the boxes.
4. a. He broke the dish.
   b. He broke the dishes.
5. a. Be sure to water the rose.
   b. Be sure to water the roses.

[___ / 5 points]

C Listen. Circle the correct word you hear in each sentence.

1. Did you **watch / wash** it?
2. How do you spell **"jeep" / "cheap"**?
3. What does **"share" / "chair"** mean?
4. How do you spell **"sink" / "think"**?
5. Did he go to **jail / Yale**?

[___ / 10 points]

Unit 15 Quiz

Name _____

Date _____   [____ / 20 points]

A Listen. You will hear a phone number or a math problem two times. Circle the letter of the set of numbers you hear.

1. a. (877) 555–9649
   b. (87) 7555–9649

2. a. (866) 555–3384
   b. (86) 6555–3384

3. a. (434) 555–5646
   b. (43) 4555–5646

4. a. $(4 \times 4) + 4$
   b. $4 \times (4 + 4)$

5. a. $10 - (2 \times 3)$
   b. $(10 - 2) \times 3$

[____ / 5 points]

B Listen. You will hear either sentence *a* or sentence *b* two times. Circle the letter of the sentence you hear.

1. a. Josh said, "My father is always late."
   b. "Josh," said my father, "is always late."

2. a. Ben whispered, "The boss will be busy all day."
   b. "Ben," whispered the boss, "will be busy all day."

3. a. Tall men, and women in raincoats, entered the bus.
   b. Tall men and women, in raincoats, entered the bus.

4. a. Plan your day and work.
   b. Plan your day – and work.

5. a. Grandma said, "Uncle Jim is clever."
   b. "Grandma," said Uncle Jim, "is clever."

[____ / 5 points]

C Commas have been removed from the following sentences. Listen. You will hear each sentence two times. Draw a slash (/) to separate the thought groups you hear.

1. Yesterday I tried to call you but you weren't home.
2. Amy wrote a letter stamped it and mailed it.
3. We ordered a hamburger two salads and some water.
4. I invited Dan but he was too busy as usual.
5. Do you want a complete dinner just a sandwich or just dessert?

[____ / 10 points]

Test and Quizzes Audio Scripts and Answer Keys

If you are reading the scripts for your students instead of playing the audio, please see the instructions in bold and in parentheses before each task.

Clear Listening Diagnostic Test

Part 1 – Vowels

Assessment CD, Track 2

(Teacher: You might want to play or read each sentence twice. Don't read the circled letters.)

Listen. You will hear either sentence *a* or sentence *b*. Circle the letter of the sentence you hear. The first one is done as an example.

1. (a.) Did you bring the bat?
2. (a.) I prefer this test.
3. (b.) It's a good bit.
4. (b.) It's on the truck.
5. (a.) The men worked hard.
6. (a.) How do you spell "scene"?
7. (a.) How do you spell "luck"?
8. (a.) We used a map.
9. (a.) Is John coming?
10. (b.) Everybody laughed.
11. (a.) I ran to school every day.

Part 2 – Consonants

Assessment CD, Track 3

(Teacher: You might want to play or read each sentence twice. Don't read the circled letters.)

Listen. You will hear either sentence *a* or sentence *b*. Circle the letter of the sentence you hear. The first one is done as an example.

1. (b.) Do you wash everything?
2. (b.) They save old bottles.
3. (b.) She loved each child.
4. (b.) We've put it away.
5. (a.) He spills everything.
6. (a.) Does she bring her card every day?
7. (a.) What does "leave" mean?
8. (a.) Who'll ask you?
9. (b.) We watch all of them.
10. (a.) He put the tickets away.
11. (b.) Is this the wrong road?

Part 3 – Number of syllables

Assessment CD, Track 4

(Teacher: You might want to play or read each word twice. Don't read the numbers to their right.)

Listen. Write the number of syllables you hear in each word. The first one is done as an example.

1. ea•sy — 2
2. clo•set — 2
3. sport — 1
4. clothes — 1
5. sim•pli•fy — 3
6. frigh•tened — 2
7. o•pened — 2
8. first — 1
9. caused — 1
10. Wednes•day — 2
11. a•rrange•ment — 3

Part 4 – Word stress

Assessment CD, Track 5

(Teacher: You might want to play or read each word twice. Make sure to stress the underlined syllables.)

Listen. In each word, one syllable is stressed more than the others. Underline the stressed syllable you hear. The first one is done as an example.

1. re<u>quire</u>ment
2. po<u>li</u>tical
3. <u>pho</u>tograph
4. pho<u>to</u>graphy
5. Ca<u>na</u>dian
6. ge<u>og</u>raphy
7. <u>Eu</u>rope
8. infor<u>ma</u>tion
9. e<u>co</u>nomy
10. eco<u>no</u>mic
11. par<u>ti</u>cipating

Part 5 – Emphasizing focus words

◎ Assessment CD, Track 6

(Teacher: Play or read the dialogue twice. Make sure to emphasize the underlined words.)

Listen. You will hear the following dialogue two times. In each sentence, one word is emphasized more than the others. Underline the emphasized word you hear. The first one is done as an example.

A: ¹ Do you think food in this country is <u>expensive</u>?

B: ² Not <u>really</u>.

A: ³ Well, <u>I</u> think it's expensive.

B: ⁴ That's because you eat in <u>restaurants</u>.

A: ⁵ Where do <u>you</u> eat?

B: ⁶ At <u>home</u>.

A: ⁷ You must like to <u>cook</u>.

B: ⁸ Actually, I <u>never</u> cook.

A: ⁹ So what do you <u>eat</u>?

B: ¹⁰ Usually, just <u>cheese</u>.

A: ¹¹ That's <u>awful</u>!

Part 6 – De-emphasizing with contractions and reductions

◎ Assessment CD, Track 7

(Teacher: Play or read each sentence twice using contractions and reductions. Accept contractions or full forms in your students' answers.)

Listen. You will hear each sentence two times. Write the missing words you hear on the blank lines. The first one is done as an example.

1. Do you think <u>she's [OR she is]</u> in her room?
2. <u>Why'd [OR Why did OR Why would]</u> you ask?
3. <u>Is her</u> work good?
4. Please <u>give him</u> the information.
5. <u>Does he</u> want food?
6. How <u>long have</u> you been here?
7. <u>What's [OR What has]</u> Matt done lately?
8. Why <u>did he</u> come so early?
9. <u>Where have</u> they gone?
10. We'd like some <u>fish and</u> vegetables.
11. They'll need <u>cups or</u> glasses.

Part 7 – Thought groups

◎ Assessment CD, Track 8

(Teacher: Play or read each sentence twice. Don't read the circled letters or the answers to the questions.)

Listen. You will hear either sentence *a* or sentence *b* two times. Circle the letter of the sentence you hear. Then answer the question that follows. The first one is done as an example.

1. (b.) "John," said my father, "is in the kitchen."
   Question: Who was speaking?
   <u>my father</u>

2. (a.) The president shouted, "That reporter is lying!"
   Question: Who shouted?
   <u>the president</u>

3. (b.) She wants pie and apples.
   Question: What does she want?
   <u>pie and apples</u>

4. (b.) Would you like a soup or salad?
   Question: What were you offered?
   <u>a soup or salad</u>

5. (a.) We used wooden matches to start the fire.
   Question: What was used to start the fire?
   <u>wooden matches</u>

6. (b.) He sold his house, boat, and car.
   Question: How many things did he sell?
   <u>three</u>

Unit 1 Quiz

A

Assessment CD, Track 9

(Teacher: You might want to play or read each word twice. Don't read the numbers to their right.)

Listen. Write down the number of syllables you hear in each word.

1. entertain   3
2. support   2
3. invented   3
4. pleased   1
5. confused   2

B

Assessment CD, Track 10

(Teacher: You might want to play or read each sentence twice. Don't read the circled letters.)

Listen. You will hear either sentence *a* or sentence *b*. Circle the letter of the sentence you hear.

1. (b.) They listed all their tasks.
2. (b.) Eric and Fred planted vegetables.
3. (a.) They need money.
4. (b.) The fans applauded their team.
5. (b.) Florence and Kay printed their ads in the daily paper.

C

Assessment CD, Track 11

(Teacher: Play or read each sentence twice. Don't read the checked columns to their right.)

Listen. You will hear a sentence two times. Mark *Past* or *Present* for each sentence you hear.

	Past	Present
1. We start work on time.		✓
2. We planned everything for her.	✓	
3. I need the money.		✓
4. We painted our house red.	✓	
5. Paul and Lisa want some new books.		✓

Unit 2 Quiz

A

Assessment CD, Track 12

(Teacher: You might want to play or read each word twice.)

Listen. Circle the word you hear.

1. (got)
2. (site)
3. (feed)
4. (rat)
5. (cut)

B

Assessment CD, Track 13

(Teacher: You might want to play or read each sentence twice. Don't read the circled letters.)

Listen. You will hear either sentence *a* or sentence *b*. Circle the letter of the sentence you hear.

1. (a.) If she's not careful, she's sure to fail.
2. (b.) Of course we should add her.
3. (a.) Which men do you mean?
4. (b.) Did you say "bit"?
5. (a.) How do you spell "beast"?

C

Assessment CD, Track 14

(Teacher: Play or read each sentence twice. Don't read the words to their right.)

Listen. You will hear a sentence two times. Circle the correct word you hear in the sentence. Then on the blank line, write the word from the box that has the same vowel sound as the word you circled.

1. I found the (pin.)   is
2. Where are the (beads)?   tea
3. The man's (cap) fell on the floor.   pan
4. Is that a new (cot)?   top
5. Tell us about your (plane).   cake

Test and Quizzes Audio Scripts and Answer Keys   93

Unit 3 Quiz

A

Assessment CD, Track 15

(Teacher: You might want to play or read each word twice. Make sure to stress the underlined syllables.)

Listen. Underline the stressed syllable you hear in each word.

1. su<u>stain</u>
2. con<u>fuse</u>
3. <u>prob</u>lem
4. be<u>gan</u>
5. <u>sen</u>sitive

B

Assessment CD, Track 16

(Teacher: You might want to play or read each sentence twice. Make sure to emphasize the words in bold and stress the underlined syllables.)

Listen to the sentences. Underline the stressed syllable you hear in each word in bold.

1. That store is too **ex<u>pen</u>sive**.
2. They live in **<u>Wash</u>ington**.
3. We believe there's too much **pol<u>lu</u>tion**.
4. We're flying to **Bra<u>zil</u>**.
5. That's a good **ap<u>proach</u>**.

C

Assessment CD, Track 17

(Teacher: Play or read each sentence twice. Make sure to stress the underlined syllable in the words in bold. Don't read the words to their right.)

Listen. You will hear each sentence two times. Underline the stressed syllable you hear in each word in bold. Then on the blank line, write the word from the box that has the same vowel sound as the peak vowel in that syllable.

1. The wedding will be **<u>out</u>side**.   _ice_
2. What is the best **<u>meth</u>od**?   _ten_
3. They signed an **a<u>gree</u>ment** today.   _tea_
4. Please don't **dis<u>tract</u>** me.   _pan_
5. We want to see a **pa<u>rade</u>**.   _cake_

Unit 4 Quiz

A

Assessment CD, Track 18

(Teacher: You might want to play or read each word twice. Make sure to reduce the vowels with the slash.)

Listen. Draw a slash (/) through the vowel that is reduced to schwa. Each word has one schwa sound.

1. seas/o/n
2. /a/ppeal
3. camp/u/s
4. prom/i/se
5. c/o/mplain

B

Assessment CD, Track 19

(Teacher: You might want to play or read each sentence twice. Don't read the circled letters.)

Listen. You will hear either sentence a or sentence b. Circle the letter of the sentence you hear.

1. (a.) I can make it.
2. (a.) Jeff said he can do it.
3. (b.) Can't you give me a ride?
4. (b.) She can't open the door.
5. (a.) The driver can be there by three.

C

Assessment CD, Track 20

(Teacher: Play or read each sentence twice. Make sure to reduce the vowels with the slash.)

Listen. You will hear each sentence two times. Draw a slash (/) through the vowel that is reduced to schwa in each word in bold. Each word has one reduced vowel.

1. You need to **conc/e/ntrate** harder.
2. This **phot/o/graph** is excellent.
3. What's her **tel/e/phone** number?
4. They live in **Washingt/o/n**.
5. Those **wom/e/n** work in the embassy.

Unit 5 Quiz

A

Assessment CD, Track 21
(Teacher: You might want to play or read each word twice. Make sure to stress the underlined syllables.)
Listen. Underline the stressed syllable you hear in each word.

1. reflection
2. inspection
3. statistic
4. practical
5. present

B

Assessment CD, Track 22
(Teacher: You might want to play or read each sentence twice. Make sure to stress the underlined syllables in the words in bold.)
Listen to the sentences. Underline the stressed syllable you hear in each word in bold.

1. We need an **electrician**.
2. That's a silly **generalization**.
3. He has strong **photographic** skills.
4. That student is studying **history**.
5. I **object** to that remark!

C

Assessment CD, Track 23
(Teacher: Play or read each sentence twice. Make sure to stress the underlined syllable in the words in bold. Don't read the columns to their right.)
Listen. You will hear each sentence two times. Underline the stressed syllable you hear in each word in bold. Did you hear a noun or a verb for the word in bold? Mark *Noun* or *Verb* next to the sentence.

	Noun	Verb
1. Did you say "**record**"?	✓	
2. How do you spell "**rebel**"?		✓
3. What does "**import**" mean?	✓	
4. Did you say "**suspect**"?	✓	
5. How do you spell "**present**"?		✓

Unit 6 Quiz

A

Assessment CD, Track 24
(Teacher: You might want to play or read each sentence twice. Make sure to emphasize the underlined words.)
Listen. Underline the focus word you hear in each sentence.

1. You sing beautifully.
2. I can't find my keys.
3. We can't see it.
4. Are you angry with them?
5. I don't believe you.

B

Assessment CD, Track 25
(Teacher: Play or read the dialogue twice. Make sure to emphasize the underlined words.)
Listen. You will hear the dialogue below two times. Underline the focus word you hear in each sentence.

Two Politicians Arguing

First Politician:	[1] The public just doesn't agree with you.
Second Politician:	[2] But my position is quite clear!
First Politician:	[3] It doesn't seem clear to the public.
Second Politician:	[4] Then maybe the public should listen better!
First Politician:	[5] And maybe they don't want to!

C

Assessment CD, Track 26
(Teacher: Play or read each sentence twice. Make sure to stress the circled syllable in the underlined words.)
Listen. You will hear each sentence two times. Underline the focus word you hear in each sentence. Then circle the stressed syllable in the focus word.

1. My cat refuses to eat fish.
2. I can't believe it!
3. He's a terrible driver.
4. This is a truly sudden decision.
5. That's an enormous expense!

Unit 7 Quiz

A

Assessment CD, Track 27
(Teacher: You might want to play or read each sentence twice. Make sure to reduce the crossed-out words.)
Listen. Draw a line through the reduced structure word you hear in each sentence. Each sentence has one reduced structure word.

1. She wants eggs ~~and~~ toast.
2. Where ~~will~~ you put that?
3. She ~~is~~ sure to be famous someday.
4. Will ~~he~~ be here?
5. Has anyone seen ~~him~~?

B

Assessment CD, Track 28
(Teacher: Play or read each sentence twice. Don't read the second line of the items.)
Listen. You will hear a sentence two times. Each sentence will have a contracted form. Circle the letter of the full form of the contraction you hear.

1. We're shut down this month.
   (a.) We are

2. I've put it away.
   (a.) I have

3. We'll be pleased to help.
   (b.) We will

4. What've you put in the soup?
   (a.) What have

5. They'll cut the bread.
   (a.) They will

C

Assessment CD, Track 29
(Teacher: Play or read each sentence twice using contractions or reductions. Accept contractions or full forms in your students' answers.)
Listen. You will hear each sentence two times. Write the missing words you hear on the blank lines.

1. He's [OR He is] working hard.
2. Is he busy?
3. No, she's [OR she is] not going.
4. They've [OR They have] already gone.
5. Who's [OR Who is] coming to the party?

Unit 8 Quiz

A

Assessment CD, Track 30
(Teacher: You might want to play or read each sentence twice. Don't read the circled letters.)
Listen. You will hear either question *a* or question *b*. The underlined word in each question is the focus word. Circle the letter of the question you hear.

1. (b.) Is it a big <u>dog</u>?
2. (b.) Was it a <u>tall</u> woman?
3. (a.) Who <u>wrote</u> that?
4. (b.) Is the <u>bear</u> hungry?
5. (b.) Where's <u>my</u> cheese?

B

Assessment CD, Track 31
(Teacher: Play or read the dialogue twice. Make sure to emphasize the underlined words.)
Listen. You will hear the dialogue below two times. Underline the focus word you hear in each sentence.

Jan: [1] I <u>love</u> to exercise!

Jim: [2] I <u>don't</u>.

Jan: [3] But exercise is <u>important</u>!

Jim: [4] Yes, but I <u>hate</u> exercising.

Jan: [5] Then you should try playing a <u>sport</u>.

C

Assessment CD, Track 32
(Teacher: Play or read each question twice, emphasizing the underlined words. Don't read the answers in the second line of the items.)
Listen. You will hear a question two times. Underline the focus word in each question. Then circle the letter of the answer that best fits the focus of each question.

1. Did the dog hurt his <u>paw</u>?
   (b.) No, he hurt his jaw.

2. Was it an old <u>man</u>?
   (b.) No, it was an old woman.

3. Did <u>you</u> say that?
   (a.) No, my brother said it.

4. Are you <u>leaving</u> at 10:00?
   (b.) No, I'm arriving at 10:00.

5. Is that John's <u>report</u>?
   (b.) No, it's his textbook.

Unit 9 Quiz

A

◎ Assessment CD, Track 33

(Teacher: You might want to play or read each dialogue twice. Make sure to emphasize the underlined words.)

Listen to the dialogues below. Underline the focus word you hear in each B's response.

1. A: Did you put the key on the desk?
   B: No, I put it <u>in</u> the desk.

2. A: I don't think that's right.
   B: It <u>is</u> right.

3. A: Did you do that work?
   B: No, <u>he</u> did it.

4. A: We serve salad or soup.
   B: I want salad <u>and</u> soup.

5. A: You look tired.
   B: I <u>am</u> tired.

B

◎ Assessment CD, Track 34

(Teacher: You might want to play or read each sentence twice. Make sure to read the circled words with the full or contracted form, as they show in the answers.)

Listen. Each sentence will have a full form or a contraction. Circle the form you hear.

1. (We are) taking the bus to work.
2. (I'm) ready to leave.
3. (They've) seen you at the mall.
4. (She is) ready to go.
5. (We'll) study your report.

C

◎ Assessment CD, Track 35

(Teacher: Play or read the dialogue twice. Make sure to emphasize the underlined words.)

Listen. You will hear the dialogue below two times. Underline the focus word you hear in each sentence.

A: [1] When is the next <u>bus</u>?
B: [2] <u>Which</u> bus?
A: [3] The bus to the <u>mall</u>.
B: [4] But there are <u>two</u> malls.
A: [5] I didn't <u>know</u> that. I want to go to the <u>best</u> one.
B: [6] Do you mean the best <u>quality</u>? Or do you mean the best <u>prices</u>?
A: [7] I want quality <u>and</u> low prices.
B: [8] Then you would have to take <u>two</u> buses.

Unit 10 Quiz

A

◎ Assessment CD, Track 36

(Teacher: You might want to play or read each word twice.)

Listen. Circle the word you hear.

1. (case)
2. (right)
3. (nose)
4. (relates)
5. (yet)

B

◎ Assessment CD, Track 37

(Teacher: You might want to play or read each sentence twice. Don't read the circled letters.)

Listen. You will hear either sentence *a* or sentence *b*. Circle the letter of the sentence you hear.

1. (b.) Did you hang the caps up?
2. (a.) Turn the light off when you leave.
3. (b.) Please put your instruments away.
4. (b.) Did you ask about the stocks yesterday?
5. (a.) Did she finish her plan on the economy?

C

◎ Assessment CD, Track 38

(Teacher: Play or read each sentence twice. Don't read the columns to their right.)

Listen. You will hear a sentence two times. Mark *Singular* or *Plural* for the last word you hear in each sentence.

	Singular	Plural
1. Did you say "nights"?		✓
2. Where did you put the tools?		✓
3. I can't find the manual.	✓	
4. Do you need more paint?	✓	
5. How do you spell "house"?	✓	

Unit 11 Quiz

A

Assessment CD, Track 39

(Teacher: You might want to play or read each word twice.)

Listen. Circle the word you hear.

1. (Dave)
2. (liar)
3. (expire)
4. (failed)
5. (debt)

B

Assessment CD, Track 40

(Teacher: You might want to play or read each sentence twice. Don't read the circled letters.)

Listen. You will hear either sentence *a* or sentence *b*. Circle the letter of the sentence you hear.

1. (b.) Don't fear the animals.
2. (a.) Did you dent this car?
3. (a.) We admired you.
4. (b.) This bell is broken.
5. (b.) We don't have any limes.

C

Assessment CD, Track 41

(Teacher: Play or read each sentence twice using contractions and reductions. Accept contractions and full forms in your students' answers.)

Listen. You will hear a sentence two times. Write the missing words you hear on the blank lines.

1. We'll [OR We will] go tomorrow.
2. Who'd [OR Who did OR Who would] they invite to the party?
3. Where'd [OR Where did OR Where would] you stay on your vacation?
4. They'll [OR They will] study in the library.
5. I said I'd [OR I would] help you.

Unit 12 Quiz

A

Assessment CD, Track 42

(Teacher: You might want to play or read each word twice.)

Listen. Circle the word you hear.

1. (rice)
2. (half)
3. (raising)
4. (view)
5. (sip)

B

Assessment CD, Track 43

(Teacher: You might want to play or read each sentence twice. Don't read the circled letters.)

Listen. You will hear either sentence *a* or sentence *b*. Circle the letter of the sentence you hear.

1. (b.) What blue ice!
2. (a.) What are the prizes?
3. (a.) How do you spell "teethe"?
4. (b.) How do you spell "very"?
5. (a.) Whose van is it?

C

Assessment CD, Track 44

(Teacher: Play or read the dialogue twice. Don't read the numbers before each line. Make sure the /z/ sound is clear in the circled words.)

Listen. You will hear the dialogue below two times. Circle the five words you hear that end in the /z/ sound.

Ann: ¹ My brother likes (fries).
Carol: ² (Does) he like them with anything?
Ann: ³ Oh yes, with (bananas).
Carol: ⁴ (Is) that the only odd combination?
Ann: ⁵ Well, he also likes (peaches) and ketchup.

Unit 13 Quiz

A
⊚ Assessment CD, Track 45
(Teacher: You might want to play or read each word twice.)
Listen. Circle the word you hear.

1. (proof)
2. (fuzz)
3. (lap)
4. (sag)
5. (kid)

B
⊚ Assessment CD, Track 46
(Teacher: You might want to play or read each sentence twice. Don't read the circled letters.)
Listen. You will hear either sentence *a* or sentence *b*. Circle the letter of the sentence you hear.

1. (a.) What's in the bag?
2. (b.) We wrote on the bus.
3. (b.) Did you say "half"?
4. (a.) Everyone loves peas.
5. (a.) Please call me "Ms. Martin."

C
⊚ Assessment CD, Track 47
(Teacher: Play or read each sentence twice. Don't read the sounds to their right.)
Listen. You will hear a sentence two times. Circle the correct word you hear in each sentence. Then on the blank line, write the consonant sound symbol for the last sound of the word you circled. Use these sound symbols: /s/, /z/, /d/, /t/, /b/, /p/, /g/, or /k/.

1. There's something in my (eyes)! ___/z/___
2. What does "(rode)" mean? ___/d/___
3. Where's the yellow (cap)? ___/p/___
4. How do you spell "(debt)"? ___/t/___
5. Please define "(gab)." ___/b/___

Unit 14 Quiz

A
⊚ Assessment CD, Track 48
(Teacher: You might want to play or read each word twice.)
Listen. Circle the word you hear.

1. (mash)
2. (path)
3. (chip)
4. (Joe)
5. (yet)

B
⊚ Assessment CD, Track 49
(Teacher: You might want to play or read each sentence twice. Don't read the circled letters.)
Listen. You will hear either sentence *a* or sentence *b*. Circle the letter of the sentence you hear.

1. (a.) Did you watch the match?
2. (b.) Write your name on the pages.
3. (a.) Put the books in the box.
4. (b.) He broke the dishes.
5. (b.) Be sure to water the roses.

C
⊚ Assessment CD, Track 50
(Teacher: You might want to play or read each sentence twice.)
Listen. Circle the correct word you hear in each sentence.

1. Did you (watch) it?
2. How do you spell "(jeep)"?
3. What does "(chair)" mean?
4. How do you spell "(sink)"?
5. Did he go to (Yale)?

Unit 15 Quiz

A

Assessment CD, Track 51

(Teacher: Play or read each phone number or math problem twice. Make sure to pause at the parentheses and hyphens. Don't read the circled letters.)

Listen. You will hear a phone number or a math problem two times. Circle the letter of the set of numbers you hear.

1. (a.) (877) 555–9649
2. (b.) (86) 6555–3384
3. (a.) (434) 555–5646
4. (a.) $(4 \times 4) + 4$
5. (b.) $(10 - 2) \times 3$

B

Assessment CD, Track 52

(Teacher: Play or read each sentence twice. Make sure to pause at the commas. Don't read the circled letters.)

Listen. You will hear either sentence *a* or sentence *b*. Circle the letter of the sentence you hear.

1. (b.) "Josh," said my father, "is always late."
2. (a.) Ben whispered, "The boss will be busy all day."
3. (a.) Tall men, and women in raincoats, entered the bus.
4. (b.) Plan your day – and work.
5. (a.) Grandma said, "Uncle Jim is clever."

C

Assessment CD, Track 53

(Teacher: Play or read each sentence twice. Make sure to pause slightly at each slash.)

Commas have been removed from the following sentences. Listen. You will hear each sentence two times. Draw a slash (/) to separate the thought groups you hear.

1. Yesterday / I tried to call you / but you weren't home.
2. Amy wrote a letter / stamped it / and mailed it.
3. We ordered a hamburger / two salads / and some water.
4. I invited Dan / but he was too busy / as usual.
5. Do you want a complete dinner / just a sandwich / or just dessert?

Glossary

alphabet vowel sound Alphabet vowel sounds are pronounced like the names of the English vowel letters **-a-, -e-, -i-, -o-,** and **-u-**. The alphabet vowel sounds are /eʸ/ (c**a**ke), /iʸ/ (t**ea**), /aʸ/ (**i**ce), /oʷ/ (c**o**ne), /uʷ/ (bl**ue**). (compare *relative vowel sound*)

combination sound A combination sound is made by combining a stop sound with a continuant. Examples: /tʃ/ (**ch**eap), /dʒ/ (**j**unk)

consonant sound A consonant sound is made by bringing the tongue close enough to some part of the mouth to produce pressure. (compare *vowel sound*) Examples: /s/ (**s**ea), /t/ (**t**oo), /l/ (**l**ow)

content word Content words – like nouns, verbs, and adjectives – carry the most information in a sentence and usually can bring a picture to mind. (compare *structure word*) Examples: "bike," "run," "green."

continuant sound A continuant sound is made by leaving an opening for air to flow from the mouth or the nose. A continuant sound can last as long as the speaker has air to continue it. (compare *stop sound*) Examples: /l/ (te**ll**), /n/ (fa**n**), /f/ (sa**f**e), /θ/ (ba**th**)

contraction Auxiliary verbs and the word "not" are often shortened and connected to the word that comes before them. This shortened form is called a "contraction." Examples: "I'll," "can't"

contrast The vowel in the most important syllable in a word (the stressed syllable) is made extra long and extra clear, while other syllables are pronounced less clearly. This contrast in length and clarity makes the important syllable easier to hear. The primary stress of the most important word in a thought group (the focus word) is made extra long and clear and is said with a pitch change. This also creates a contrast, so that the important word can be noticed more easily.

emphasis Emphasis is the way native English speakers highlight the most important words in what they say (the focus words) to show a contrast with less important words. Emphasis is added to a word by making the stressed syllable extra long and clear and adding a pitch change. Example:

We're all w**ai**ting for you.

focus word A focus word is the most important word in a thought group. Focus words are emphasized with a pitch change and a long, clear vowel in the stressed syllable to help the listener notice them. Example:

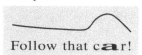
Follow that c**a**r!

off-glide After the main sound of the alphabet vowel sounds, the tongue moves up to provide an after-sound (e.g., the second part of /eʸ/). It is shown in the book by the little superscript /ʸ/ or /ʷ/.

pitch pattern This is the musical change in the voice, up or down, that helps the listener notice the important words (focus words). Example:

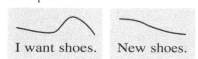
I want shoes.   New shoes.

relative vowel sound Relative vowel sounds are the vowel pronunciations that do not sound like the names of the vowel letters. (compare *alphabet vowel sounds*) Examples: /æ/ (p**a**n), /ɛ/ (t**e**n), /ɪ/ (**i**s), /ɑ/ (t**o**p), /ʌ/ (c**u**t)

rhythm Rhythm is the pattern of long and short syllables.
□□▭ □ □ ▭
Example: absolute   Have some fruit.

schwa Schwa (/ə/) is the reduced vowel sound. It is very short and very unclear. By reducing less important syllables in a word to schwa, the most important syllable (the stressed syllable) is made more noticeable. Example:

banana   bən**a**nə

sibilant Sibilants are consonant sounds that make a hissing sound. This hiss comes from air rushing through a narrow valley along the speaker's tongue. A sibilant is a type of continuant. Examples: /s/ (hi**ss**), /z/ (bu**zz**), /ʃ/ (ma**sh**)

stop sound A stop sound is made by stopping the airflow in the mouth so that the sound cannot continue. (compare *continuant sound*)
Examples: /**t**/ (sa**t**), /**d**/ (sa**d**), /**p**/ (ca**p**)

stress The stressed syllable is the most important part of a word. It is mainly shown by lengthening the vowel and making it extra clear.
Examples:

Africa ▲frica   Alaska Al▲ska

structure word Structure words – like pronouns, articles, and prepositions – do not carry as much information as content words, and they do not bring a picture to mind. They are usually not emphasized. (compare *content word*)
Examples: "the," "in," "will"

syllable A vowel itself, or a group of sounds with a vowel in the center. Syllables are the basic element of English rhythm.
Examples: Tom (1 syllable), a•tom (2 syllables), a•to•mic (3 syllables)

thought group A thought group is a group of words that belong together to make sense. They are often clauses or phrases or just short sentences. There is usually one focus word in each thought group.
Example: "I want **tea** and a tuna **sand**wich."

vibration Vibration is the rapid, regular motion of the vocal cords that produces voicing.

vocal cords The vocal cords are a structure in the throat that can vibrate to produce a voicing noise. The vibration can be felt by placing your hand on your throat while making a voiced sound or listening while closing your ears.

voiced sound Voiced sounds are made as the vocal cords vibrate. (compare *voiceless sounds*)
Examples: /**v**/ (lea**v**e), /**z**/ (bu**zz**), /**b**/ (**b**at), /**g**/ (**g**oat)

voiceless sound Voiceless sounds are made without vibration of the vocal cords. (compare *voiced sound*)
Examples: /**f**/ (lea**f**), /**s**/ (bu**s**), /**p**/ (**p**at), /**k**/ (**c**oat)

vowel sound A vowel sound is made by not letting any part of the tongue touch any part of the inside of the mouth. A vowel sound is the most important part of a syllable. (compare *consonant sound*)
Examples: /**i**^{y}/ (s**ee**), /**e**^{y}/ (s**ay**), /**o**^{w}/ (g**o**)

whisper "Whisper" means to speak very quietly and without any voicing.

Bibliography

Acton, W. 2001. Integrated English speaking skills. In J. Murphy and P. Byrd (eds.), *Particular approaches: Specialists' perspectives on English language instruction.* Ann Arbor: University of Michigan Press. pp. 197–217.

Acton, W. 1991. Changing fossilized pronunciation. In A. Brown (ed.), *Teaching English Pronunciation: A Book of Readings.* London: Routledge. 120–135.

Allen, V. 1971. Teaching intonation, from theory to practice. *TESOL Quarterly* 4 (1): 73–81.

Avery, P., and S. Ehrlich (eds.). 1992. *Teaching American English Pronunciation.* Oxford: Oxford University Press.

Ballmer, T. 1980. The role of pauses and suprasegmentals in a grammar. In H. Dechert and M. Raupach (eds.), *Temporal Variables in Speech.* The Hague: Mouton. pp. 211–220.

Bell, A. G. 1916. *The Mechanisms of Speech.* New York: Funk & Wagnalls.

Bolinger, D. 1986. *Intonation and Its Parts.* Stanford: Stanford University Press.

Brown, G. 1977, 1990. *Listening to Spoken English.* London: Longman.

Brown, G. 1978. Understanding spoken language. *TESOL Quarterly* 12: 271–284.

Carney, E. 1994. *A Survey of English Spelling.* London, New York: Routledge.

Celce-Murcia, M., D. Brinton, and J. Goodwin. 1996, 2010. *Teaching Pronunciation: A Reference for Teachers of English to Speakers of Other Languages.* New York: Cambridge University Press.

Chela de Rodriguez, B. 1991. Recognizing and producing English rhythmic patterns. In A. Brown (ed.), *Teaching English Pronunciation: A Book of Readings.* London: Routledge.

Chun, D. 2002. *Discourse Intonation in L2: From Theory and Research to Practice.* Amsterdam: John Benjamins.

Cutler, A., and D. Norris. 1988. The role of strong syllables in segmentation for lexical access. *Journal of Experimental Psychology: Human Perception and Performance* 14 (1): 113–121.

Dalton, C., and B. Seidlhofer. 1994. *Pronunciation.* Oxford: Oxford University Press.

Dauer, R. 1993. *Accurate English.* Upper Saddle River, NJ: Prentice-Hall.

David, D., L. Wade-Wooley, J. Kirby, and K Smithrim. 2007. Rhythm and reading development in school-age children: A longitudinal study. *Journal of Research in Learning to Read* 30 (2): 169–183.

Ferber, E. 1940. *A Peculiar Treasure.* New York: Doubleday.

Forster, E. M. 1924. *A Passage to India.* New York: Harcourt.

Fry, D. 1955. Duration and intensity as physical correlates of linguistic stress. *Journal of the Acoustical Society of America* 27: 765–768.

Fucci, D., M. Crary, J. Warren, and Z. Bond. 1977. Interaction between auditory and oral sensory feedback in speech regulation. *Perceptual and Motor Skills* 45: 123–129.

Gilbert, J. B. 2012. *Clear Speech From the Start: Basic Pronunciation and Listening Comprehension in North American English* 2nd ed. New York: Cambridge University Press.

Gilbert, J. B. 2001. Six pronunciation priorities for the beginning student. *The CATESOL Journal* 13 (1): 173–182.

Gilbert, J. B. 1999. Joseph Bogen: Clarifying the wine (implications of neurological research for language teaching). In D. Mendelsohn (ed.), *Expanding Our Vision: Insights for Language Teachers.* Oxford: Oxford University Press.

Gilbert, J. B. 1995. Pronunciation practice as an aid to listening comprehension. In D. Mendelsohn and J. Rubin (eds.), *A Guide for the Teaching of Second Language Listening.* San Diego: Dominie Press.

Gilbert, J. B. 1994. Intonation: A guide for the listener. In J. Morley (ed.), *Pronunciation Pedagogy and Theory.* TESOL:3–16.

Gilbert, J. B. 1987. Pronunciation and listening comprehension. In J. Morley (ed.), *Current Perspectives on Pronunciation: Practices Anchored in Theory.* TESOL: 29–40.

Goswami, U., and P. Bryant. 1990. *Phonological Skills and Learning to Read.* Psychology Press. Hove.

Grant, L. 2010. *Well Said: Pronunciation for Clear Communication* 3rd ed. Boston: Heinle & Heinle.

Hahn, L. 2004. Primary stress and intelligibility: Research to motivate the teaching of suprasegmentals. *TESOL Quarterly* 38 (2): 201–223.

Hatch, E. 1977. Optimal age or optimal learners? *Workpapers in Teaching English as a Second Language* X: 45–56.

Kjellin, O. 1999. Accent addition: Prosody and perception facilitate second language learning. In O. Fujimura, B. D. Joseph, and B. Paled (eds.), *Proceedings of Linguistics and Phonetics Conference 1998.* The Karolinum Press, Prague. 2: 373–398.

Klatt, D. 1975 Vowel lengthening is syntactically determined in connected discourse. *Journal of Phonetics* 3: 139.

Krashen, S., M. Long, and R. Scarcella. 1979. Age, rate, and eventual attainment in second language acquisition. *TESOL Quartely* 13: 573–582.

Leahy, R. M. 1980. A practical approach for teaching ESL pronunciation based on distinctive feature analysis. *TESOL Quarterly* 14: 209–306.

Lehiste, I. 1977. Isochrony reconsidered. *Journal of Phonetics* 5: 253–263.

Levelt, W. 1989. *Speaking: From Intention to Articulation.* Cambridge, MA: MIT Press.

Miller, S. 2000. *Targeting Pronunciation.* Boston: Houghton-Mifflin.

Morley, J. 1992. *Rapid Review of Vowel & Prosodic Contexts.* Ann Arbor: University of Michigan Press.

Morley, J. 1991. The pronunciation component in teaching English to speakers of other languages. *TESOL Quarterly* 25 (3): 481–520.

Munro, M., and T. Derwing. 2011. The foundations of accent and intelligibility in pronunciation research, *Language Teaching.* Cambridge University Press, 44 (3): 316–327.

Ohala, J., and J. B. Gilbert. 1981. Listener's ability to identify languages by their prosody. *Studia Phonetica* 18: 123–132.

O'Malley, M., D. Kloker, and B. Dara-Abrams. 1973. Recovering parentheses from spoken algebraic expressions. *IIEE Transactions on Audio and Electro-Acoustics*, AU-21: 217–220.

Patel, A. 2008. *Music, Language, and the Brain.* Oxford: Oxford University Press.

Pickering, L. 2001. The role of tone choice in improving ITA communication in the classroom. *TESOL Quarterly* 35 (2): 233–256.

Pribam, K. 1980. The place of pragmatics in the syntactic and semantic organization of language. In H. Dechert and M. Raupach (eds.). *Temporal Variables in Speech.* The Hague: Mouton. pp. 13–20.

Wade-Wooley, L., and C. Wood. 2006. Prosodic sensitivity and reading development. *Journal of Research in Reading* 29: 253–257.

Wennerstrom, A. 1991. *The Music of Everyday Speech: Prosody and Discourse Analysis.* Oxford: Oxford University Press.

Wood, C. 2006. Metrical stress sensitivity in young children and its relationship to phonological awareness and reading. *Journal of Research in Reading* 29: 270–287.